HOHENASPERG:

An American boy betrayed by his Government during World War II

by

ARTHUR D. JACOBS
Born in the U.S.A.

Copyright © 1999 Arthur D. Jacobs. All rights reserved.

Published by
Universal Publishers/uPUBLISH.com
USA • 1999

ISBN: 1-58112-832-0

www.upublish.com/books/jacobs.htm

Cover photograph: Author at age thirteen

Dedication

In memory of a son, brother, and father gone home, Archie Keith Jacobs (1953-1976), killed in the line of duty in Morton County Kansas

In tribute to
Viva Sims Jacobs
David and Michael Jacobs
Dwayne Jacobs
Dianna and Whitney Hatfield
Paul J. Jacobs
Lambert W. Jacobs
Edwin and Mary Simmons

And in memory of
Lambert D. and Paula (Knissel) Jacobs
Art and Mildred (Wilson) Dreyer
John Wade and Roxie (Allred) Sims

A salute to the Crew of the S.S. Aiken Victory on the January 17, 1946 voyage, and to the WWII GIs who came to my rescue

CONTENTS

Acknowledgements

It is with regret that I cannot acknowledge all who have encouraged and helped me through the years to write this story. First I owe a special debt to my wife, Viva, my three children, David, Dwayne, and Dianna, and to my three grandchildren, Paul, Michael and Whitney. Each in his or her own way, have allowed me the time, encouraged me, inspired me, and at times humored me through this process.

A special note of thanks to my colleague and friend Joseph E. Fallon who listened to and believed in my quest for truth, and who for six years has steadfastly helped me with my research.

I am ever indebted to William (Bill) J. Hopwood, Commander, USNR, Retired, who has for the past ten years encouraged me to write this book. Bill, here it is.

To my brother, Sonney (Lambert), I say thanks for allowing me to jog your memory, as painful as it may have been. To his wife, Barbara, thanks for your words of encouragement and editing skills.

To Priscilla Young, my neighbor, thanks for editing the initial manuscript. And to all of my friends and associates in Tempe, Arizona who cheered me on, I say thanks.

To Larry Landon, Major, U.S. Army Retired, for sharing his circa 1946 photographs of the Place, Hohenasperg, Camp 76.

To Stanley W. Schmucker formerly (1945) a member of the U.S. Army's 291st Field Artillery Battalion stationed at Hohenasperg, who shared with me a booklet about

Hohenasperg written by Edward Bierman a corporal in his platoon there.

To Andreas Zack for helping me with technical translations, for providing me with present-day photographs of Hohenasperg; and for encouraging me to publish this work.

To David Woods, a friend and former student, thank you for being a test "market" for your generation.

My thanks to my friend and colleague, Professor David H. Lynch of Arizona State University, for reading and editing the manuscript.

Last, but not least, I thank my friend and colleague, Professor Dwayne A. Rollier of Arizona State University. Thanks Dwayne for being a buddy. Thanks Patty for praying and sharing.

Preface

Almost fifteen years ago, while I was watching a national television broadcast, the following words were spoken: "During World War II the U.S. Government did not intern German Americans." The program's subject was the internment of Japanese Americans. I sat back and thought to myself, "Have I been dreaming all these years that I was interned in a camp with Japanese Americans? I know I played with them. Some of my friends went to school with them. I even went swimming with them, and dined with them. I was behind the same barbed wire fences that were being discussed."

Then, on August 16, 1984, The Honorable Norman Y. Mineta, a U.S. Representative from the State of California, in his testimony before a subcommittee of the United States Senate said, "We did not lock up German-Americans." While reading newspaper reports and editorials from around the country, I read, "German Americans were not interned." I was perplexed and became convinced that a misinformation campaign was in place. These and other untrue statements about the internment of Americans of German descent inspired me to write my story.

Statements like Congressman Mineta's, "We did not lock up German-Americans," are paradoxical. Were Mineta and others telling the members of the United States Senate and the world that if German-Americans had been locked up, then the internment program would have been justified, or were they so misinformed that they did not know that German Americans were interned?

In 1945, I was told by my seventh grade teacher in Brooklyn, New York, and by my parents that internment was part of war and what was happening to my family was supposedly being done in the best interests of the country. I had even heard officials of the U.S. Government tell this to my parents. Because what I heard, read, and viewed in the 1980s conflicted with what I was told in the 1940s, I began to search for the truth about the World War II civilian internment program of the United States of America.

During this research my friends, acquaintances, colleagues, students, and librarians would ask, "What are you researching?" After they learned the "what," they asked "Why?" Usually I replied, "It is a long story about the early years of my life." "You see," I said, "I was interned in the United States." The astonished reply generally has been, "You were interned? I thought only Japanese Americans were interned." I responded promptly, "Not true. I am not a Japanese American, but I am an American of German descent, who was interned at Ellis Island, New York; Crystal City, Texas; and at the prison called Hohenasperg (Camp 76), Germany."

This book documents the "long story." It is based on my research and recollections of the events that took place. It tells of the devastating effects that the decisions and actions of a judicial system gone awry had on one family—the Lambert D. Jacobs family of 411 Himrod Street, (Ridgewood) Brooklyn, New York, U.S.A.

Arthur D. Jacobs
Tempe, Arizona
March 24, 1999

Introduction

This book tells the story of Arthur D. Jacobs. It begins in 1943 when, as a ten-year-old boy, agents of the Federal Bureau of Investigation invaded and ransacked his family's home on three separate occasions based solely on anonymous accusations. The book then charts how the U.S. Department of Justice repeatedly violated his family's constitutional rights:

In violation of the Sixth Amendment, the author's father was denied the right "to be confronted with the witnesses against him..." (Although World War II ended more than half a century ago, the FBI, claiming national security considerations, has refused repeated requests by the author to know the identity of his father's accusers.)

In further violation of the Sixth Amendment, the author's father was denied the right "to be informed of the nature and cause of the accusation..."

In violation of the Fourth Amendment, the author's family was denied the right "to be secure in their persons, houses, papers, and effects, against unreasonable searches and seizures..."

In violation of the Fifth Amendment, the author's parents were denied the right that "No person...shall be compelled in any criminal case to be a witness against himself..."

In further violation of the Fifth Amendment, the author and his family were denied the right that "No person...shall be deprived...of property, without due process of law..."

These violations culminated in the repatriation of the Jacobs family to a war ravaged and starving Germany in 1946, where the U.S. Occupation Authority imprisoned them. This book is a story of injustice and self-discovery.

For over four decades, Arthur D. Jacobs had accepted the official position that the "internment of aliens of enemy nationality" was necessary for public safety and national security during times of war. As a result of almost two decades of research, however, he has discovered that this was not the sole reason for the internment program under the Roosevelt Administration.

In his opinion, one of the primary purposes of the internment program was to provide the U.S. Government with leverage in negotiations with Berlin for the return of persons from the Americas who were interned by Third Reich.

In February 1944, at least 634 German Americans were shipped to Nazi Germany as part of this exchange program. In January 1945, two months after the author's father was interned, another exchange voyage occurred.

A subtle, but important, aspect of internment was the mindset of the internees, themselves. Because internment challenged their belief in the integrity of the U.S. justice system, internees adopted, as a psychological defense mechanism, two contradictory views of American justice. Based on interviews with several former internees and discussions with his father and mother, the author learned most internees thought, "I did nothing to deserve to be interned, but I wonder what 'Hans' did. Why is he in here? He must have done something, because in America you are not arrested unless you violated the law."

In recent years, the author has discussed his father's case with several journalists. Invariably at the close of those discussions the journalists would say, "Now Art, you know your father must have done something wrong. In America, we don't go around arresting people without cause." Art's consistent reply has been, "Prove it! Show me the cause! Saboteurs, spies, and other agents of the enemy were not interned; they were either sent to prison or executed." Unable to show cause, the journalists respond with only shrugged shoulders.

The deeper the author delved into the internment program, the clearer it became to him that most, if not all, of those who were interned did not pose a threat to national security. Many were interned on the basis of anonymous accusations. For example, neighbors and even the man on the street, would tell FBI agents that a person has a picture of Hitler in his or her house, or was a contributor to the Nazi Party. The FBI added such information to the alien's FBI dossier with little or no attempt to confirm the truth or accuracy of the accusations.

That internment was not completely motivated by national security considerations can be seen in the case of the author's father. Despite both the unanimous opinion of the local hearing board and the legal opinion of the U.S. Attorney for the Eastern District of New York that the author's father should not be interned, Edward J. Ennis, Director of the Alien Enemy Control Unit of the Department of Justice had him interned. In view of the two exchange voyages previously noted, there is a strong indication that the author's father was interned to become a member of an internee pool for possible future exchanges.

This book, however, transcends the story of the injustices inflicted on the author and his family. It is a cautionary tale, which reveals that during wartime the rights guaranteed to us by the U.S. Constitution can become tenuous.

If during wartime the U.S. Government can deny the constitutional rights of one citizen, the constitutional rights of every citizen are in jeopardy. Once the precedent is established, the authorities may apply it as frequently and as broadly as they desire. If it could be done to German Americans yesterday, it can be done to Arab Americans or Serbian Americans today. Just because what happened to the author occurred over fifty years ago, do not assume that it cannot happen today, tomorrow or to you. Many of the laws that enabled the Justice Department to violate the constitutional rights of the author's family are still on the books.

The author is confident that the U.S. Government will finally acknowledge what it did to German Americans between 1941 and 1948. He hopes that after reading his book, Americans will recognize that their rights can be threatened by unconstitutional acts carried out by officials of their government. Remember, "the price of liberty is eternal vigilance."

Joseph E. Fallon
Free lance writer/researcher
March 1999
Rye, New York

Chapter One

A Place

God was with me in this place.

It is *a place* that has had many names and has had a presence for centuries. Some have called it a hill, a hump, a mountain. It rises almost 1,200 feet. It is *a place* that was used to imprison poets, economists, other political prisoners, soldiers, and persons with tuberculosis. The Nazis murdered Jews here. Terrorists have been imprisoned here. It is surrounded by an abysmal and wide moat followed by towering walls. It is *a place* that was not clean or well lit.

It is *a place* of many names. Two examples are:

> **Tränenberg**—the mountain of tears, and
> **Höllenberg**—the mountain of hell.

It is said of this *place* that those who go up the hill do not come back. It is a short fifteen-minute drive from Ludwigsburg, a thirty-minute drive from Stuttgart, and a ninety-minute drive from Nuremberg. Its official title is Hohenasperg also known as Hohen Asperg.

It is a place of nightmares, not a place of pleasant dreams. I remember this place, and how I feared it. When I was but thirteen, I was a prisoner and *celebrated* my thirteenth birthday there. It is there that I became a teenager, and was harassed and threatened. In 1972, twenty-six years after I was released from this place, I drove by it. From a distance it came into view, but I did not stop. I really wanted to stop, but I could not. As I went by I thought, I just can't go back up that hill. I was reminded of the cold, damp cell, and I remembered the hangman's tree. I began to relive my life in this place and my years of nightmares about it.

Visions of the large tree, the hangman's tree, in the courtyard flashed through my mind. I remembered being told by my guard, an American soldier, that those who do not obey orders are hung; and if that doesn't work, they're shot! He said, "See the bullet marks in the tree!" My prison "mates" included high-ranking German officers suspected of war crimes and other persons who were being "denazified." As I passed the place, I said, "That's the place where I was thrown into a prison cell." I heard a cell door being shut— with a thunderous bang! I thought, I was just a kid and wondered why was I treated like a criminal in that place? I remember that each time I attempted to tell the soldier, "I am an American," he would respond, "Shut up, you little Nazi, shut up!"

For almost four decades I questioned my memory about the hangman's tree. I repeatedly asked myself, "Was there really a hangman's tree in that place?" Did I dream it? Were there bullet marks on the hangman's tree? Did I also imagine those other horrible things? Anytime I was out of my cell I was under the watchful eyes of armed guards. Did I dream that my armed guard shouted, "Do you see that big tree in the courtyard, it's the hangman's tree?" "Make sure," the soldier said, "that you don't ever take your hands off the top of your head when you are out of your cell." The guards escorted me to and from my cell for each meal. I was required to eat in a standing position, with armed guards all around me, staring at me, whispering among themselves. I, the prisoner, was required to be silent. I was ever reminded by my guard not to talk to other prisoners while I was eating. He reminded me that I was to eat in silence; and when I was finished, to stand there with my hands on my head until I was ordered to move on. Several times, I blurted out, "Sir, I am an American!" The soldier snapped back, "Shut up, you

6

Nazi! Remember what I told you about the hangman's tree."
As usual, I became frightened and stood there, speechless.

Chapter Two

The Cell

Even though I was a kid, I was locked in a cell in this place. I asked myself many questions. What did I do to be treated like this? I had no idea why Americans would treat another American so harshly. I was just a kid! Was I dangerous? Why was I yelled at? Why did they call me a "little Nazi?" It was cold, wet, and dreary in my cell—it was stark! It was beyond scary. It was frightening. It was madness. Why did my fellow Americans, soldiers in the United States Army, shout orders at me? I am not a Nazi; I am an American, I thought to myself. Why didn't I have papers that proved I was an American? I believe I was able to keep my sanity only because I always searched for a mental escape from the horrors I was facing. Thus, during my stay in this place, I would have flashbacks. How did I get here?

I remembered the ride in the tarpaulin covered U.S. Army Studebaker truck (called a "six by six" by the American soldiers), that took us up the hill to this place. Then I recalled the viehwagen (boxcar) in which I was sealed for almost four days during one of the coldest winters on record, without heat, without blankets, and without toilets, except for an open, stinking bucket. I remembered I curled up in a fetal position in an attempt to keep myself warm. It is a wonder I did not freeze to death. Each time the train stopped, I would hear the armed American GIs bark "Raus, mach schnell," in their broken German. Why did they shout at me in German, I wondered? I was an American, I understood English. Didn't they know that I was an American? My thoughts wandered back to when I left the ship that brought us to Germany.

8

I thought about my fifty-mile trip in the rear of the army truck, the "six by six" that took us (about 25 persons in the truck I was in) from the ship at the port of Bremerhaven to the city of Bremen. It did not look like a city. It was just a huge pile of rubble. We passed one pile of rubble after another. Where buildings once stood, now there was nothing but heaps of bricks and mortar—ruins. In some instances there were only walls standing amidst the destruction caused by the bombing and fire bombing of the city, mile after mile the scene was the same. I could see what looked like old women pulling hand wagons in which they had placed the bricks they had picked from the piles of rubble. They would put the bricks in the wagon, pull the wagon to where bricks were stacked, and then they would take each brick out of the wagon, one by one, and place it neatly on the stack. I had a good view from where I sat at the very back of the truck. You might say I had "the best seat in the house." I was ordered to sit there by the armed military guard. I can still hear the loud flapping of the truck's tarpaulin. I remember the cold wind whipping in from the back end, while I sat there almost frozen. The winds whipped into and around me. I thought my feet were going to freeze off! I hung on to my seat the best I could as the driver sped over the cobblestone roads and swerved to miss the potholes. And when the truck hit a pothole, I nearly bounced out, but somehow I managed to hold on. Why, I wondered, was I ordered to sit at the very back of the truck? As we passed one section of the city, there were no buildings, not even shells or walls of structures—nothing—just rubble, and at a distance in the background stood a tall bomb shelter. It appeared undamaged. Then I said, "My God, what happened here? How many people died here?" However, my thoughts in the cell were short-lived.

My mind continuously wandered from the past to the present. What have they done with my mother? What have they done with my father? What have they done with my brother? Where are they? My thoughts turned back to the reality of the moment, to me. Each time the soldier escorted me back to the cell, there was silence as I entered. Then the soldier slammed the door shut. Wham! What a noise! The bang of steel against steel thundered through the cell and made me shudder. Each time I returned to my cell it seemed like this banging noise became louder and louder, and my nerves became more frazzled. I heard him set the key in the latch and lock it. In my cell it was painful to dwell on the present for very long periods of time. Where did all of this begin? Where will it end? The thoughts of misery, destruction, carnage, and hate were too much for my young mind to bear. I would have to think of better times, better places, and better people. My mind wandered back to my family, friends, teachers, and neighbors in Brooklyn.

Chapter Three

The Best of Times, The Worst of Times

I often wondered about my friends in Brooklyn. What is my best friend Fred Flynn doing now? Did Fred's brothers get safely back from the war? Is everyone together again? Who is helping the Italian grocer on the corner of my block? I worked for him, stocking his shelves, and bringing up the bottles of beer and sodas from the cellar beneath his store. I even helped to make deliveries to his customers. Many times he or his son would take me to the fresh vegetable market, where they purchased produce for the store. Sometimes he would even let me use the *picker* to get the cereal boxes from the top shelf. Anytime the grocer needed help I was available. I wondered if his sons had to go off to war? There was also the German butcher's shop across the street. Once in a while the butcher would allow me to sweep up the sawdust from the floor of the shop, and my reward would be a slice or two of lunchmeat. Both of these proprietors were friends of my parents.

I also did odd jobs for the coal and kerosene man whose business was in a small garage on Cypress Avenue. He would let me fill his customers' kerosene cans (heating oil) and/or their coal sacks. There were times when he let me go on major deliveries with him to help put the coal chute into the cellars of his customers. He, like the grocer and the butcher, was a nice man—each of them rewarded me well for my work. I was always looking for ways to earn money so I could buy the things I needed that otherwise we could not afford.

Besides doing these small jobs, I formed the Himrod Street baseball team. When we were starting out, I told all of our players to get their numbers and shirts, and bring them over to my house and my Mom would sew on the numbers. Then I told Mom what I had planned. She replied, "You did what?" I said, "Mom, I told them you would sew on their numbers. You know Mom, I figured because you sewed all day at work, you could do it fast." Mom saw the excitement in my eyes and agreed to do it. Thus, the Himrod Street Gang was the only sandlot baseball team in the neighborhood with numbers on their shirts. Our team had no coach and no equipment. We just played sandlot ball with our own gloves, balls, and bats. We were also the umpires, which led to many arguments about balls and strikes. Sometimes we had to cover our worn-out baseballs with adhesive tape, and some of our cracked baseball bats were mended with either adhesive or black electrical tape. I do know this, we had lots of fun. I missed my friends.

From time to time my friends and I would sneak into the Grover Cleveland High School baseball field. When we played there, each of us had a dream. A dream that one day we too would play baseball for Grover Cleveland High School. Then, we would no longer have to slip into the ballpark. However, when I left my home in Brooklyn, my dreams stayed behind. I no longer had visions of playing for Grover Cleveland.

I began to think of my Pop. I remembered how honest he was, and how he taught us to be honest. Two particular lessons on honesty came to mind.

One lesson on honesty occurred when I was eight years old. During one of my early ventures, I walked down to a Woolworth's "five and dime" store on Knickerbocker Avenue about eight blocks from my home. I saw a pencil and eraser I thought I really needed, but I didn't have enough money. I looked and saw no one watching, so I grabbed them and put them quickly in my pocket. My heart was racing as I walked out of the store. When no one shouted or ran after me, I became proud of myself. I had done it! I would not let myself think about it being wrong. It was only a pencil and eraser! That evening shortly before dinner my father asked me how I got my new pencil and eraser. I replied, "Oh, the manager in the five and dime store gave them to me." "Which, five and dime store?" Pop asked. I replied, "Oh, you know the Woolworth Store on Knickerbocker Avenue." Pop replied with another question, "Are you sure?" I said, "Yes, I'm sure." Then to my surprise, Pop said, "Let's go down there so you can show me." "Okay," I said. Instantly, I became very nervous, but I figured after we went down the three flights of stairs from our flat, Pop would believe my story. Wrong! Pop and I walked down to the store; all during our walk Pop kept asking me if I was sure that the manager gave me the pencil and eraser. Each time he would ask, I replied in the affirmative.

When we got to the storefront, Pop said, "Let's wait out here. When you see the manager who gave you the pencil and eraser, point him out." All along my thinking was that my father was bluffing, and I was going to stick to my story, because I knew the consequences if Pop found out that I stole the pencil and eraser. When I saw a manager, I turned to my father and said, "Pop, there he is, the young man in the white shirt and black tie. That's him!" Pop looked at me and said, "Okay, let's go in and talk to him." I was caught and I knew it. I turned to my father and told him that I took them without paying. This, I thought would close the case. But it did not. Instead my father looked at me and said, "Archie, go in there and give back the pencil and eraser to the manager, and tell him you're sorry for stealing and that you won't steal ever again." The walk to the manager seemed like ten miles! But he was very nice and when I handed them to him and explained what I had done, he said, "Thank you for being honest." I learned a valuable lesson.

My second lesson regarding "honesty is the best policy" occurred when I was ten and a paperboy for the <u>Brooklyn Eagle</u> newspaper. On this Sunday morning I started my route early as usual. It was still dark. I picked up my papers just a few doors from where I lived. When I was sorting my papers and putting them into my newly won canvas delivery sack, I noticed a bicycle parked in front of some garages across the street.

When I finished my route and came around the corner, the bike was still there. I had never ridden a bike before, but I always wanted to try, and wanted a bike for my paper route. I took my delivery sack and threw it into our vestibule, then I went back to the bike. I got on it and to my surprise in a very short time I was riding the bike quite well. It was getting late in the morning and I thought I had better get home before my father came looking for me. I rode the bike just up the street to where our flat was and parked it in our yard. Then I went into our apartment house and down into the cellar. I unlocked and propped the cellar door open, and walked the bike down the cellar steps and parked it in front of our storage stall.

After I closed the outside cellar door I anxiously ran up the stairs, I could hardly wait until I told my father about my latest find. By the time I got upstairs to our flat I was a bit winded, but quickly announced my finding with a question, "Pop, guess what I found?" Pop asked, "What did you find?" I replied, "A bicycle." "A what?" he asked. I again told him I found a bicycle. Then my father got up from his chair and asked me, "And just where did you find the bike?" I told him by the garages on the other side of our street. "Take that bike back where you found it immediately! Make sure you leave it just as you found it! And from now on when you find something that isn't yours, leave it alone."

"But, Pop," I said. "No 'buts,' take it back," Pop ordered. So I took it back. I thought the whole episode would be over and done with after I took back the bicycle, but it was not. When I got home I was lectured by my father about "finding" things that don't belong to me.

As I thought about my wonderful Pop, I became sad. Why did they treat him like that? It was almost too disturbing to think about. I began to wish that this is just a nightmare and when I wake up we will still be in Brooklyn all together as a family. But this nightmare was real!

I also thought about my days in the Boy Scouts of America. I remembered learning to tie the hangman's noose. I never thought that I would ever worry about being hung in such a noose. It was most difficult for me to tie some of the knots, while others I found easy. One reason I found it hard to tie some of them was because the instructors were right handed and I was a lefty. The sheepshank and the fisherman's knot came to mind. My brother and I would walk together to our scout meetings that were held in the Lutheran Church about eight blocks from our home.

Suddenly and without warning I was startled by a strange sound! It sounded like an echo in a tunnel. I was distracted, and asked myself, "When did this disaster begin?"

The Summer of 1943 was the beginning of the nightmare. One day, two Special Agents of the FBI rapped on the door to our flat. I remember the loud rapping startled me and that my mother was very frightened. She went to the door and asked, "Who is it?" The agents announced, "The FBI!" My mother unlocked and opened the door and before my 4' 9" mother could invite the agents in, they flashed their badges and identification cards and forced their way in. They told my mother and me to sit down in the kitchen while they searched our home. The agents not only searched our home, they also ransacked it! They threw the clothing and other articles out of my dresser and made a shambles of my room. Clothing and other articles were scattered all over the house.

The agents found nothing, but they did take several of my mother's personal photographs of her two brothers. In addition to the photographs, the agents took several letters that my parents had received from my father's parents in Germany. Before they left, my mother had tears running down both of her cheeks. It was clear that she had been frightened by these men and what they had done inside her clean, neat home. Neither my mother nor I knew why the agents had been in our home and why they tossed our clothing and other personal effects out of the dressers. They just came in and took over. They asked no questions, offered no apologies, and gave no reason for the search.

When the agents finally left, my mother sobbed and cried aloud. She questioned why this had happened. It took quite awhile, but she slowly pulled herself together and without a word began to put everything back in place.

All of a sudden reality set in again—the present—I was back in my cold and damp cell. I wonder where my mother is? Is she also in a cell like this at another place? Is it as cold and damp where she is held? Do they shout and bark out commands to her, as they do to me. Where is my brother? Where is my father? What is happening to them?

Each time I was in my cell by myself, it seemed as if it was an eternity before I would see or hear anyone, and when the armed soldier came for me, I again shuddered. He would begin by shouting, "Put your hands on your head." Then he would unlock the cell. "Come out!" he would shout. As soon as I stepped out of the cell, he would yell, "Stop!" The GI would direct me as I walked, and would follow just a few paces behind me, telling me when to turn, when to stop, and when to go. This happened each time I went to eat. When I ate I was not to turn my head to the left or the right, but only look straight ahead. And when I had finished, he would say, "Get your hands on top of your head." And as usual he gave me my marching directions and orders. As I marched back to my cell he reminded me of the hangman's tree. It would be a relief, I thought, to get back to my cell. Once I was back in the cell, however, I anticipated the moment when I would be getting out of the cell once again. I did not like it in or out of the cell. It was difficult to concentrate, and I could not focus. My mind wandered. I sat, stood, or lay waiting nervously, expecting the next commands. I thought, just over one year ago I was in Brooklyn. What events brought me here? What am I, an American, doing here?

My mind once again returned to the thoughts of home. When I left Brooklyn a part of me remained there, and ever since we left, there has been a missing link in my life. That missing link is the lost friendships, never to be renewed.

I even missed having the neighbors tell us that we should not play baseball or stickball in the street. There was little traffic then, but there was always the danger of a ball being hit through a window—this did happen on occasion. My dad had to pay for a window or two broken by my brother or me.

Then my thoughts were shattered by the ritual roll call, the bang on my cell door, and a voice that shouted, "Are you there?!" To which I was required to respond, no matter what time of day or night, "Present!" If my response was not loud or clear enough for the soldier, he would say, "Can't hear you, speak louder." The roll call visits brought me back to reality, to the cold, damp, dreariness, and loneliness of my cell. Roll call was either just plain harassment or the commander had to find something for his soldiers to do or both. "What am I doing here, why am I here, where is this place?" I have to get this place out of my mind. I can go

17

crazy here or I can be hung. I must return to pleasant thoughts.

Mr. Brill was my seventh grade teacher at P.S. 81 in Brooklyn when I left to be interned. Over and over I am reminded as to what Mr. Brill said to me before I left. When I told him that I was leaving to be interned in a family camp in Texas, he said to me, "Archie, don't concern yourself with this, these things happen during wartime. These days will pass." I thought, what does he mean by saying, "These days will pass?" His words stuck with me and, in part, they helped me to survive this ordeal. Those words gave me hope.

I held Mr. Brill in high esteem. I seem to remember that he was a veteran of the U.S. Army Air Corps, who had gone to war and was back in his teaching profession. Mr. Brill did not talk about the war in our classroom. However, I did notice something about him that was different than most teachers. Even though he was as stern and strict as another favorite teacher of mine—Mrs. Lewis—Mr. Brill connected with his students. He did not appear to be as serious about trivial matters as my other teachers. He had a quality about him that I did not understand then. Now I know that Mr. Brill was a student's teacher.

During my last day in his class, Mr. Brill once more admonished me, in private, not to take this internment thing too seriously; it's just part of war. Repeatedly he said, it's just part of war. It was a sad day for me when I walked out of Mr. Brill's class for the last time. I thought to myself, if Mr. Brill knew how I was being treated here in this prison, I know he would come to my rescue and stop this un-American act. He was a true American. The actions taken by some government officials that brought about this situation were un-American. Mr. Brill would not approve. FBI agents and other officials had harassed my father. On several occasions they attempted to have my father confess to something that he did not do. They grilled him time and time again. Each and every time, he would cooperate, for he had nothing to hide. He had committed no crime, had harmed no one, and he supported the American war effort. Despite this harassment my father did not complain, and he reminded us that in war strange things happen. Like Mr. Brill, my father knew these days would pass.

If Mr. Brill knew of my trip in the boxcar, I asked myself, "What would he do about it?" I am sure he would agree with me that this is no way to treat a person—a boy, regardless of his ethnicity. If he had been in charge he would not have allowed the soldiers to lock us in the boxcar. He would not have allowed the troops to tell the women to squat in front of them to relieve themselves on the ground. And if Mr. Brill had been the commander of this prison, his soldiers would not have threatened to hang or shoot a young boy. He would not have permitted one or more of his solders to call a young patriotic American boy a "Nazi." Mr. Brill knew I was a patriot and that I had worked for the American war effort. He knew I collected more than three tons of scrap paper. He knew I purchased U.S. Savings Stamps. He knew I donated our only family radio to the American Veterans Rehabilitation Post. Disabled veterans were being trained in radio repair, and when the call came for radios, I persuaded my parents that we should donate our radio. My parents agreed. Mr. Brill would understand. He would have compassion. There was no compassion in this place. Mr. Brill would have claimed that the treatment my family and I had been receiving was disgraceful—un-American—he would have been outraged. I was reminded, "This day too will pass."

My thoughts went back to my trip to Germany. I did not want to leave the ship, and this voyage to end. In ten short days, the ship had become my home, and several of the merchant seamen had become my brothers. I had grown attached to them. Another set of friendships would soon be split. In less than a year this had happened four times.

As soon as we docked in Germany and I stepped onto the deck it was so cold I shivered. As I was going down the ship's gangplank I noticed a host of armed guards, complete with rifles and pistols. I did not know whether these soldiers were guarding the ship or if they were there to protect us. I soon learned it was neither.

All at once, I had the impression that I was about to leave joy and step into misery. As we neared the end of the gangplank, the soldiers started giving orders like, "Move it! Move it! Move it!" While several of the soldiers shouted such orders, they would also point their rifles towards us and then point them in the direction we were to go. First, they lined us up, and we stood there freezing. No one seemed to care that we were freezing, frightened, and fearful of the unknown. My teeth began to chatter! I got colder and colder, but still no action was taken. Decisions were either not being made, or we were being punished. Was it retribution? We continued to wait for what seemed like hours. Finally, some canvas-covered army trucks pulled up, and we were immediately ordered into the trucks. As one truck filled up, the rest of us were marched to the next truck. And so it went until all of us were loaded. Sitting inside the waiting truck was not as cold as it had been while standing on the ground. The tarpaulin top provided some relief from the elements. My mind was full of questions. What brought me here? Why are we being treated this way? Don't these soldiers understand that some of us are Americans? We are not criminals! We are not dangerous!

I was startled by a loud noise somewhere in the prison. It was hard to concentrate in my small, damp cell. In a few days it would be my thirteenth birthday. Just two years ago I was celebrating my eleventh birthday in Brooklyn. I could hardly really remember what it was like, because shortly after my birthday there was another visit of the FBI to our home. The FBI agents ransacked and searched my mother's well-kept household for a second time. This time she almost went into shock. And once more, the FBI came up empty-handed. No contraband—cameras, guns, or short-wave radios. No propaganda pamphlets promoting the Third Reich. No picture of Hitler hanging in my father's bedroom! This must have been a great disappointment to the agents, and by now they must have been frustrated. Despite not finding anything, a few days after this forced entrance, my father was arrested, fingerprinted, photographed, and then placed on parole pending a hearing. In August, the FBI paid a third visit to our home, and again came up empty-handed.

As I continued to think about past events, I realized it was more comfortable in this cell than it was in the truck that was used to transport us to Bremen. Once we left the ship we were treated like cattle instead of humans. First, I was forced to stand outside in the freezing weather. Second, they put me in the back of a truck next to the tailgate. When traveling, the wind whipped into where I was sitting. Adults, including my father, volunteered to sit in my place, but a soldier denied these requests. The soldier wanted a child on the last seat in the truck because a child would be least likely to try to escape. Third, after the truck ride, I was transported for ninety-two hours in a boxcar and only fed bread and water for the entire journey. And then after all this, they put me in prison—A Place—Hohenasperg also known as the U.S. Seventh Army, Camp 76 Internment Facility.

The boxcar was freezing and dark—pitch black! I had never heard of people being transported in boxcars. It smelled of body odor, urine, and human feces. Did I just hear the screams of a woman? It can't be. There are no women in this prison. I remember! When the soldier slammed the

21

boxcar door shut for the first time, one of the women screamed at the top of her voice, "Oh please, please don't shut the door! I'm scared! I can't stand it!" she shouted. Then she began to cry. And every now and then, she would shout, "Someone please help me!" Her husband, as well as the other women and men in the boxcar, attempted to soothe and comfort the frightened woman, but it was no use. During the next ninety-two hours in the boxcar, these sounds would often be repeated. When the woman began to scream I plugged my ears with my fingers to blot out the sound. I tried to sleep, but I was too cold, too frightened. There were few words spoken and the silence in the boxcar was eerie. I could not decide which was worse, the screams of the woman or the eerie silence. The train was rather slow, and there would be a thump, pause, thump. It sounded as if the train was lumbering its way down the tracks. When the boxcar shook or hit a bump, I could hear the sloshing in that nasty, sickening toilet bucket.

The coldness of my cell reminded me of the terrible coldness of the boxcar. I was thankful when I first climbed aboard the boxcar because I saw a potbelly stove inside. As soon as we were in the boxcar, several of the men built a fire in the stove. After a long day of shivering in sub-freezing temperatures, I felt warmth for the first time since we left the ship. Because I was chilled to the bone, I tried to get right next to the stove. I was told not to get too close to the stove because my clothing might catch on fire. I believe I would have sat on the stove if they had let me!

One of the men said, "You know, we are locked in here and there is no way out, so we must be careful." We would take turns sitting as close to the stove as was safe. "Heat at last," I said to myself. After the train pulled away from the siding where we were loaded, several persons complained that the stove was not hot enough. Then, one of the men stoked the fire, and added more coal. A few minutes later I noticed that the walls of the stove began to glow red. I felt the heat even though I was sitting further away than I had been earlier. I wondered about the glowing sides of the stove. I had seen the top of our stove in Brooklyn glow before, but not its sides. Some of the women continued to complain that they were freezing and wanted more heat. Again, a man stoked the fire and added more coal. The red glow of the stove became more pronounced. I became concerned.

One of the men shouted at the man stoking and fueling the fire, "Mensch![1] What are you doing, the stove is already glowing red-hot, and you're still adding coal. Do you want to catch this boxcar on fire?" This was followed by a serious discussion among the adults. Then I observed one of the men touch his cigarette to the side of the stove and presto, it was lit. The discussion regarding how hot the stove should be went on for a few more minutes. Tempers even flared during the discussion, including my father's, but this was short-lived. Finally, an agreement was reached that we would not allow the fire to get the stove red-hot.

It had been a long day, and I had just dozed off, when I was awakened by what seemed to be distant screams of, "Fire! Fire!" At first, I thought I was dreaming. The train continued to lumber along. A few moments later, I thought I heard faint banging sounds amidst the screams. Then, without warning one of the men in our boxcar shouted "Fire!" Someone said, "What do you mean, fire?" He said, "Be quiet! Listen!" No one made a sound. Everyone listened intently. Then we heard more clearly, the banging noise and the shouting of, "Fire! Fire!" made by the people in the boxcar ahead of us. We went to the back of our boxcar and began to bang on the wall while we shouted, "Fire!" It was a panic situation. We pounded and pounded

---

[1] Translated: Man!

on the wall of the boxcar wall, while we continued to yell, "Fire!" at the top of our lungs. We did this for several minutes before the train finally stopped. Even after the train stopped we continued banging and shouting. Finally we heard our door being unlatched, and only then did we stop the pounding and yelling.

The armed soldiers slid the door open, shined a flashlight into the boxcar, stood there with their weapons in the ready position, and one soldier asked, "Where is the fire?" Someone from our boxcar replied, "Not here, I think it is in the next boxcar." A soldier, while continuing to hold his weapon in the ready position, stood in front of the door to our boxcar. The other soldiers moved on. Then we could hear, "Raus! Get out! Mach schnell!" repeated over and over again. The only thing I could see was the soldier who was standing by the door of our boxcar and what appeared to be the rays of spotlights coming from both ends of the train.

The soldier guarding us remained silent. A few minutes later, I heard an officer tell the soldiers to tell the "Krauts" that there will be no more fires in the stoves. All fires were to be extinguished and the coal removed from the boxcar. "Why?" someone asked. After a few moments of silence the soldier said, "I don't know." Then an officer appeared, shined his flashlight into our boxcar and looked in. He said, "You will have to douse the fire in your stove, someone will bring you a bucket of water." Again someone asked, "Why?" The officer responded, "Because the people in the next boxcar got the stove so hot it caught the wall of the boxcar on fire." A soldier appeared with a bucket of water, handed it to one of the men, who poured it into the stove. The stove gave off steam and I could hear the steam's hissing sound. Finally, the fire in the stove was completely doused. The man who doused the fire was told to put the remainder of the coal into the bucket and then give the bucket to the soldier. After this was done, the soldier promptly slammed the door to our boxcar shut, and latched it. Again, we were sealed in the boxcar. For the rest of the trip, more than three days, we had no heat, despite the sub-freezing weather.

The train stopped many times during the ninety-two hour trip, presumably to take on water. I had no idea why or where the train stopped—but it was never in sight of buildings—I only remember open landscape, dark gray skies, and cold weather.

The first morning we stopped it was quite early, and daylight had just broken. As the train ground to a halt, I heard one or more of the adults say, "Why are we stopped? What is going on?" There was no sound outside. I think this silence was frightening to all of us. It was almost pitch black inside the boxcar, so you could not see what others were doing. One or two people would say, "Shh!" when someone would talk. Then after a few minutes, we heard footsteps, then the footsteps stopped. Again silence. Then for a short while there was complete silence on the inside and outside of the boxcar. The next thing I heard was the door being unlatched. It was as if the person unlatching the boxcar door was attempting to gain access without disturbing anyone. Again, silence. All of a sudden, wham, the door was shoved open with a bang. It sounded as if all the boxcar doors were shoved open simultaneously. Outside our door stood an armed soldier with his weapon pointed at us. It seemed as though what happened to us then was something that had been trumped up by the enemy, the Third Reich, not by Americans.

The soldier directly in front of our boxcar door and the other soldiers up and down the track shouted in unison, "Raus! Get out!" All of us were stiff and slow to move. The soldier

25

kept saying "Raus, mach schnell!"[2]   We were groggy, frightened, cold, and still we had to lift ourselves up off the floor.   Then, still in somewhat of a daze, one by one we headed for the open door.   What little body warmth I had generated in the boxcar was instantly gone.   It was not easy to get from the boxcar to the ground, and the men had to help the women and children get out.   The two-inch sized gravel surrounding the tracks and on the ground below the boxcar were dark and light gray.   When I jumped down I slipped on the gravel, but luckily I was not hurt.   Others were not so fortunate.   This turned out to be our so-called rest stop. Some internees asked, "Why are you doing this to us?" To which one or more of the soldiers responded, "Shut up!"

We stood or squatted, shivering in what must have been sub-zero temperatures, waiting for the next set of orders. There were at least four sets of soldiers guarding us. About ten paces to the east of the boxcar, facing the door to our boxcar, there was a line of soldiers standing holding their semi-automatic carbines across their chest.   At each end of the boxcar a soldier stood armed with a carbine and a forty-five-caliber pistol.   On the other side of the boxcar, there was another line of soldiers of whom you could only see their legs, but presumably they too were armed.   On top of the boxcar, there were yet more soldiers standing with their firearms in the ready position.

Many times I have thought back to my days in the boxcar, and said to myself, "We must have been very dangerous to have been so heavily guarded, even though about two-thirds of us were either children, infants or women."   My father always said jokingly about the incident, "They were just protecting us from the enemy."

---

[2] Translated: Out, hurry up

When the soldiers were ready to go, they would shout, "Get back in, mach schnell!" Everything we did had to be in a hurry-up mode. Back in we would go, and again the men would have to help the women and small children into the boxcar, but my brother and I could boost ourselves up. All during the re-boarding time I heard, "Mach schnell!" Once all of us were in the boxcar, a soldier would slam the door shut, then latch it and lock it. For what seemed like hours the train would not move. Lying or sitting in the dark boxcar in silence and having no idea what was going to happen next again scared all of us. I know I was more frightened while the train was idle than when it was moving, because my young mind imagined the worst. So it was a relief for me when the train began to move. At least I knew that we had not been completely forgotten and left there to freeze to death.

Without warning, there was another reality check! My hope faded as the armed soldier banged on my cell door, and said, "Time to go." Chills went over my entire body. I was terrified. I knew we would again have to pass the hangman's tree. Each time we passed the soldier would remind me, "Remember what I told you, if you are not good we will hang you from that tree." "Look at it!" he would shout, "Look at it!" I would turn my eyes toward the tree and immediately look back in the direction we were headed. All the time my hands were clasped on top of my head, as I had been instructed to do each time I left my cell.

Then I remembered the Friday my father was arrested by the FBI. Pop was at work at Elmhurst, when the FBI came and arrested him without notice. Pop said, "I was handcuffed and taken from the factory as if I was a criminal. I was shamed!"

That day, when Pop did not come home at his usual hour, my mother went to the front window and watched and waited, as was her practice when my father was late coming home from work. After an hour or two of just sitting there, Mom began to cry. I kept asking her, "Mom, what's wrong?" "Nothing Archie, I'm just waiting for Pop." Mom finally composed herself, set the table and we ate dinner—it was a most somber occasion. During the entire weekend after my father's arrest, my mother sat by the window, faithfully watching and waiting for Pop to come. It was not to be. By late Sunday, my mother's eyes were almost swollen shut, because she had cried almost continuously. When I asked her what's wrong, "Nothing!" was always her reply.

Finally, three days later, an Immigration and Naturalization Service officer visited our home. The officer told my mother that my father had been arrested and that he was interned at Ellis Island. We now knew that Pop was alive and well, but that he would not be coming home. Why did it take so long for the U.S. Government to notify us about the whereabouts of Pop?

The three ransacks of our home by FBI agents, and the taking away of my father was the last straw for my mother. Little did I know then, that from the day of my father's arrest forward our family life would never be the same. As a matter of fact, it was the beginning of the end of our life as a family unit.

Why was it that the efforts of some of our close friends did not win the release of my father from internment? Why didn't our pastor help to get my father released after he was arrested in Brooklyn?

.

Chapter Four

Ich bin auch ein Deutscher!

After they arrested my father, my mother asked many people what she should or could do to get her husband back. There was not a person that we knew of German heritage, that is to say, a naturalized American, who would come to the aid of my parents. At each turn, Mom and Pop hit a roadblock. Several days after we learned that my father had been arrested, Mom asked someone to have the pastor come to our home. She knew our pastor would help.

When the pastor arrived, I invited him in. We lived on the third floor in a building with six flats as they were called, three on one side of the building and three on the other, separated by a hallway and a staircase. By the time the pastor got up to our door he was panting. Mom, asked him to sit down, and offered him a cup of coffee and some cookies. Then she explained to the pastor that the FBI had ransacked her home and arrested her husband. "The FBI picked him up at his work and without notice took him to Ellis Island," she told the pastor. The pastor, like others before, asked, "Why was your husband arrested?" To which, my mother replied, "I have no idea." Mom told the pastor in every little detail about her problem as she now saw it. She told him of the first visit of the FBI agents and how they rifled through the clothing in her dressers, and threw the clothing all of over the place. She said, "The FBI treated us as if we were criminals."

My mother told the pastor that her husband was not allowed to have a lawyer at his hearing. "They only let my husband have three witnesses," she said, "and I was one of the three." Mom went on to tell him, "I told the members of my husband's hearing board that my husband and I never talk politics. I also told them that my husband would fight to defend America." "You would think," she said, "that after my husband's best friend, an American Jew, told the hearing board that he would be the first to know if my husband had any communist or Nazi party leanings, that the hearing board would not have interned my husband. But they did."[3]

Mom explained to the pastor that her two sons were in constant need of new clothing because they were growing so fast. And then there was the rent. Mom was quick to point out to the pastor, "But I did not ask you to come to ask you for financial help. I only asked you to come to help me get my husband back home. I need my husband. He is not dangerous, and the boys need their father! I have asked many people to help us," she said, "but all say that there is nothing they can do." She explained that some of the persons she had asked were naturalized American citizens of German heritage. One after the other each said, "I am a German, and if I say anything, they will arrest me too. I cannot help you."

"You," my mother said to the pastor, "can help. You know my husband. You know that he is a good citizen. You know that he has taught his sons to be American patriots and encouraged them to support the American war effort. You should be able to help us. My boys have always purchased war savings stamps at their school. My youngest son, Archie, gave our only radio to the War Veterans Rehabilitation Program. He was also commended by his

---

[3] Neither my father nor my mother ever knew that my father's Alien Enemy Hearing Board unanimously recommended that he not be interned. And this was followed up by a special letter from the U.S. Attorney of the Eastern District of New York that he agreed with the Board's "unanimous" decision to not intern my father. My mother's intuition proved to be correct.

principal for collecting more than three tons of scrap paper for the war effort. He and his brother did this all single handedly. Each Saturday, when other children were playing or at the movies, my boys would be collecting papers and sometimes even scrap iron. When their cart was full they would have to push it for a mile or more to where the scrap paper was being assembled." "Pastor," she said, "I know you can help us." In closing my mother told him, that because he was a clergyman, the government would listen to his plea on behalf of her husband and his family. Each time she paused, the pastor would take another sip of his coffee. He listened intently. I could tell from the expression on my mother's face that she thought she had finally found someone who could and would help us get Pop back home. I too was convinced that the pastor would help.

After taking another sip or two of fresh coffee that my mother had just poured, the pastor turned to her and spoke in German. I thought this was strange; I had never before heard the pastor speak German. English had always been the language in our home, so I was concerned that the pastor was speaking German. I think he talked to my mother in German because he did not think I could understand German. I knew some German, and I could understand many words. I really couldn't speak the language, although I had often practiced with my mother. When I practiced, my mother would have me describe household items like, table, chair, door, window, closet and so forth, in German. First she would describe an object in German, and then I would tell her the name of the object in English. So I did have a grasp of some fundamental words. I listened intently.

Then, the pastor in a formal and serious tone of voice, said, **"Frau Jacobs, Ich bin auch ein Deutscher. Und wenn Ich werde was sagen über dein Mann, dan werde ich auch**

arrested."[4] I was shocked, and my mother wilted. After this the pastor got up from the table without another word, said goodbye and left. What the pastor had told my mother was, that **he too was a German, and if he spoke out he also would be arrested.** The pastor feared for his own freedom. He made no apologies for his planned inaction.

After the pastor left, these words came out of my mother's mouth, words that I have always remembered, "Archie, if we cannot turn to our pastor for help, what is there left for us to do?" My mother felt defeated. This was the lowest point in her life. She knew her pastor had abandoned her. I think she could understand why other Germans abandoned us, and she could accept their inaction. However, she could not understand why the pastor deserted her, and it made her heartsick. I could tell that Mom was shaken more now, than ever before. We never heard from that pastor again.

This should not have happened to our family. The events leading to my father's arrest were contemptible and should have been so considered, by our relatives, friends, and in particular by our pastor. But there was a war going on, and the fear of retribution can often stop someone from doing the right thing. This fear was well founded because it was true that all persons, citizens and non-citizens, American-born or foreign born, would have been considered suspicious characters had they spoken in support of my father. Thus unfortunately, during World War II officials of the United States Government governed and controlled thought through fear.

Mom had lost all hope, and I did not have a clue as to what we should do. I tried and tried to console her, and I pleaded

---

[4] The Germans often used a mixed language, in this instance the pastor used the term "arrested."

with her to stop crying. Eventually her tears did stop, but I could see a deep sorrow in her face, and she looked drawn. She was sad and frightened. I told my mother that there was still hope, but often, she would respond, "Archie, it's no use." I told her that we should ask our neighbors for some ideas, and she agreed.

Our neighbors who lived in the flat across from us were retired schoolteachers. We presented them with our problem and told them that my father was imprisoned on Ellis Island. My mother told them how the FBI had ransacked her home on several occasions. Then she told them how the FBI had whisked my father away from his place of work and had him locked up on Ellis Island. They were shocked! They knew that my father was a good man and that he was patriotic. Both of the ladies suggested that my brother and I personally write a letter to the Department of Justice. They also recommended that we ask our landlord if he would write a letter to the government on behalf of our father.[5] Immediately, I took on these responsibilities.

---

[5] Letters and excerpts of letters written by others and myself are contained at the back of this book in **The Chronology** section.

Chapter Five

In the Shadow of Liberty

My brother and I always liked ferry rides. I loved to watch the gulls and smell the crisp air. We had taken ferryboats to both Staten Island and to the Statue of Liberty. I even remembered visiting the Statue of Liberty with my mother a few years earlier. We were looking forward to our ferry trip and of course the visit to see Pop. When we first boarded the Ellis Island Ferry at Battery Park, both my brother and I hurried for a seat that would give us the best view. Mom, because of her short legs, almost had to run to keep up with us. Once the Ferry left the Battery Park slip, I noticed that there were several other women on board the ferry, but I do not recall seeing other children. As we approached the island; we got a glimpse of Pop and other men, walking around in the fenced compound. All of the men, including my father, were wearing red and black plaid jackets. I waved and waved, but Pop couldn't see me. I don't think he was expecting us. While we were docking, I thought to myself, "Why is my father walking around in that yard?"

While the ferry was slowly making its way into the slip at Ellis Island, every now and then it would bump up against the pylons that appeared to help keep the ferry guided into the landing dock. While we were doing this, I kept staring at my father and the men who were walking with him on the blackened oval in the fenced compound. It was a cold and dreary day, and I thought it strange that these men were walking in circles. Some stopped walking and came to the fence, looking and waving at the ferry. Others, like my father, just kept walking. Once the ferry was docked and secured, we were ordered to disembark. We went from the ferry into a somewhat narrow hallway. After we had walked about fifty steps or so, a guard stopped us. He rifled through my mother's purse, and checked the package of cookies and cakes that she brought to my father. A matron examined each of us. After we were examined and questioned, we then turned to the right into the visitors' room. I was puzzled at what I saw.

Inside the room there were tables with partitions. On one side of a partition sat the visitors and on the other side were the internees. I had seen this scene before. It reminded me of a movie. In this movie prisoners were separated from their visitors by a partition. Guards were standing at the end of each table listening to every word that was being said and watching each and every move that was being made by both visitor and prisoner. I wondered, is my father a prisoner, like those I had seen in the movies?

My father was not in the Visitors Room when we arrived. My mother told the guard that we were there to visit Lambert Jacobs. Shortly thereafter, my father approached the partition with his big smile. It was obvious he was delighted to see us. He was dressed in army khakis, like the rest of the prisoners. After a short greeting, he gave my brother and me a candy bar; then Mom and Pop visited. I have no idea what they talked about. I do remember that the guards and matrons at the ends of the tables kept a watchful eye on both sides of the partition, and if the words of either party were inaudible, either the matrons and/or the guards would say, "Speak louder!" There was no privacy.

The time was approaching when we had to leave the island, as we had to catch the next ferry back to Battery Park. Mom began to cry when the guard told her that the visiting time was over. Pop tried to console her, by saying, "Paula, everything will be alright, take the boys and go, you must go." Just then, the guard shouted, "Visiting hours are over." A matron and a guard then escorted us back to the ferry, stopping to examine us along the way, just as we were when we entered the Visitors Room.

My brother and I again scrambled for a seat with a view, I noticed that the ladies remained at the outside of the ferry when we left the island. So I went to the outside of the ferry to see what was going on. Each lady had removed a white handkerchief from her purse, and as the ferry pulled away from the dock, they began to wave their handkerchiefs. Some of the men behind the fence did the same, and many just waved with their bare hands. I thought when the ferry leaves the slip, the women will put away their handkerchiefs. But they kept on waving. They waved long after they could no longer see their loved ones. Mom waved her white handkerchief until we were almost back to Battery Park. I was really fascinated. Each time we visited the island I saw this demonstration of love. Little did I know then that in a month or two I too would be imprisoned on this island. Then I, like my father, would be on the other side of the visitors' partition.

Back in my cell, I had a vision of those white handkerchiefs, and that vision gave me hope. I recall saying to my mother when we were on the ferry, "Mom, Pop can't see you anymore. Stop waving your handkerchief." Mom ignored my plea, and continued waving. It was some time later, after all the ladies discontinued waving their white handkerchiefs, that she said to me, "Archie, you see when all of us are waving, the men see more than the very small white spot of each handkerchief; they see a "cloud" of white. "A white cloud," she said, "that gives them hope." Whispering hope. Then I understood.

I do not think any of my friends knew that my father had been arrested. If they did know, they did not question me or talk to me about his arrest. We continued to play as usual. Sometimes we simply walked up and down the streets of the neighborhood counting "Blue Stars," and in particular "Gold Stars" in the windows. We knew that the each Blue Star "told" us that a member of the family was in the service of our country, and the Gold Star reminded us that a family member was "killed in action." In our neighborhood there were many Gold Star banners hanging in the windows. The war had taken its toll.

My father had registered for the draft, and his draft board advised the FBI that he was in compliance with the Selective Service Act. In the newspaper, I had read that the government either had or was thinking of drafting 35-year-old males with two or less children. My father had even mentioned to my mother, that he might be drafted. But my father's draft board did not call him to duty.

My father had repeatedly told the FBI and members of his hearing board that he would not want to fight against his native country Germany, because he had close relatives there. However, he did tell them that he would fight against Italy and Japan. He also said that if Germany were to invade the United States he would defend American soil. Despite those statements, the FBI and other agents of the government repeatedly asked him whether he would serve in the armed forces of the United States. I believe that had my father been called to arms by the United States, he would have proudly served with honor. Surely, if he did not intend to serve, he would not have registered for the draft.

Chapter Six

Christmas 1944

Christmas was approaching. Before Christmas Day we would take the ferry a couple of more times to visit my father on the island—Ellis Island. On Christmas Eve of 1944, which was to be the first Christmas without our father, we were in for a wonderful surprise. That evening, my parents' best friends, Ann and Dan Lipensky, appeared at our door. They wished us a very Merry Christmas, and came with a rather large gift for my brother and me. The Lipenskys (both were American Jews) knew that it was the practice at our home to open gifts on Christmas Eve. My mother said, "What a pleasant surprise, that you came to visit us. Just having you spend the evening with us is a wonderful gift." Tears welled up in her eyes.

I knew that those of the Jewish faith did not celebrate Christmas, and thus it was gratifying to me that the Lipenskys came to be with us during our celebration. Dan and Ann did everything they could to help us forget, at least for the moment, that our father was not there. As a matter of fact, Dan, who knew my father and many of his mannerisms quite well, began to act like him. We opened our gift. "Wow," I said, "an encyclopedia set." This, I thought, would help me with school projects.

Usually our father would set up our train set, but this Christmas Eve, Dan got our Lionel trains running. Mom put on the coffeepot and set the table with coffee cups and saucers. Everything had its place, and each place setting was perfect. Mom even set a place for my father.

While they were in our home, Dan and Ann gave my mother many words of encouragement. "Paula," Dan said, "these days will pass." A month or so later, I would hear my seventh grade teacher, Mr. Brill, give me these same words of encouragement. Dan went on to say, "Paula, you must not dwell on the fact that Jake is not here. Make the best of it." Between playing with my brother and me and consoling my mother, Dan and Ann were kept quite busy during that Christmas Eve of 1944. After the Lipenskys left, my mother's facial expression reflected that she had a fresh glimmer of hope, all of us did. Dan and Ann encouraged us to keep seeking ways to have my father released, and we did just that.

In late January of 1945, I wrote another letter to Mr. Ennis. In this letter I advised him that I had not heard from him in regards to my December 12, 1944 letter. This time I informed him that my mother was sick in bed. I also told him that it was most difficult for my brother and me to do without our father. In addition, I told him we needed our father home and that it was a shame for the government to do a thing like this to a father of two American boys; a father who always encouraged his sons to help the war effort.[6] Along with my letter, I enclosed two commendations that had been awarded to me through my school for my support of the war effort.

A couple of weeks later, I received a letter dated February 6, 1945 from Mr. Ennis, who said, "…no change will be made in your father's internment status at this time." This is the last time that I heard from him. At the end of that February my mother, my brother, and I were on our way to Ellis Island. This time we were not going for a visit, but to be

---

[6] Both of my letters remain on file in the records of the Department of Justice.

interned. Locked up! Even though we were voluntary internees, we would not be allowed to leave even if we changed our minds. Like several businesses in my neighborhood that were closed for the "duration of the war," we now would be locked up for the "duration." This started us on the road that brought me to my cell in Hohenasperg.

Chapter Seven

Leaving Home

My twelfth birthday was on the 4th of February. I used to remind my friends that I was born in this month, as were George Washington and Abraham Lincoln. I do not recall whether we celebrated my birthday that year. What I remember most about that particular February, is that Mom made up her mind. She was going to join her husband with or without permission from the Immigration and Naturalization Service. Mom had obtained suitcases and trunks for the type of belongings we could take with us to Ellis Island. Personal belongings that we could not take, she gave to relatives for safekeeping. I do not know how our furniture and other possessions were divided up, but on the day we left, February 27, 1945, nothing was left in our flat except our suitcases and trunks. Before we left the apartment, I turned back and took one last look.

Our flat was now empty and hollow. I reflected that the flat, our home, which had been vibrant and full of joy, was now empty, hollow, and lifeless. I turned, walked out of the apartment, locked the door, stopped once again, then went down to the second floor and gave the key to our landlord, Mr. Pardy, and said goodbye. Mr. Pardy gave me a dime, just as he had done monthly when I paid our rent, and said, "Goodbye and good luck." This was the last time I saw Mr. Pardy.

After I gave Mr. Pardy the key, I proceeded down the steps to the first floor, walked out into the vestibule and noted that our name was no longer on our mailbox. Then I went out of the front door, paused, stood on the stoop, and said to myself, "Why are we doing this?" My mother and brother were waiting.

It was late in the afternoon before we were able to leave, and it was dark when we arrived at Ellis Island. We each had one suitcase. This is what I thought remained of our possessions. However, I later learned that my mother had placed some of our clothing, cooking ware, and eating utensils in two trunks. These were placed in storage, seemingly for the duration.

My personal possessions were discarded—my train set, my baseball cards. My airplane models of the P-38 Lockheed Lightning and B-17 Bomber were gone. My bed and nightstand were also lost. What about the cart that I used to collect papers for the war effort, where is it? Does anyone collect old newspapers now? My baseball glove, bat and balls, my hockey stick, my roller skates, all those things were gone.

From the moment I walked out of our building at 411 Himrod Street until we arrived at Ellis Island that same day, my memory is blank. During our excursion to the island I must have dwelled upon what I had just left, my home, my friends, my teacher, my school, and my neighborhood. I have no recollection of our trip to Ellis Island. While this was happening, I did not know then what I now know: this would be the end of our family unit. Never again, would we be like we were before the FBI arrested my father at his place of work. There would be no more Sunday afternoons when I could watch my father read the comics and the news while he listened to the works of Beethoven, Mozart, and Bach. Through him, I learned to enjoy the classics of the great composers. Also gone forever would be the evenings nights, when as a family we would listen to the *Lone Ranger* and *Gangbusters*. My brother and I never again would sit by a radio together, doing our homework, while listening to *Jack Armstrong the All-American Boy* radio program. Mom and Pop used to say, you should first do your homework, then listen to the radio. My brother would always say he could do both at the same time. I could not. My homework came second to the radio program. Sitting on the stoop with my brother and my friends would be no more.

Gone would be the recital of the Pledge of Allegiance each day of class. No more Friday P.S. 81 assemblies in my white shirt and red tie. It would be a long, long time before I would again sing "My country 'tis of thee..." I held these moments close to my heart.

Abruptly, social life as I knew it ended. The culture I was familiar with had changed. I would no longer communicate with my childhood friends. Trading baseball cards would become a distant memory. My world as I knew it simply stopped—it ceased to exist. Playing with marbles stopped. Sitting with my friends under the lamp post during the hot summer nights ceased. It is as if I became another person overnight. This part and many other aspects of my family life ended when we left 411 Himrod Street, Brooklyn, New York, in the United States of America. Less than a year after I left my neighborhood I would find myself in a prison cell in a war-torn, starving Germany. Instead of being surrounded by my playmates, I would be surrounded by armed military guards. Guards who shouted at me, threatened me, and pointed their weapons at me. When the FBI arrested my father, little did I know that three years of my life would be taken from me.

Chapter Eight

Ellis Island—*The Isle of Tears*

As we got off the Ellis Island Ferry, several startled guards and matrons greeted us. We were unexpected "guests." They asked us who we were and told us that you could only visit during regular hours. My mother said that she was here to join her husband and had given up our home and she had no where to stay with her two sons. The officials, for whatever reason, allowed us to stay. The record shows that we were booked in at 10:00 P.M. on February 27, 1945. My brother and I were not allowed to have a room with or next to our mother, and we were assigned beds in the men's open bay sleeping quarters. Even though I was only twelve, as an internee I was considered an adult. This was another life change for me. By a stroke of an official's pen, I was no longer a child; I was classified and treated as an adult. A guard took my brother and me to the men's quarters. There we had to check out linen, and make our beds. Our beds were in the same hall as Pop's, but not next to his or next to one another. My father showed us around and introduced us to several internees. He showed us the public latrines, a string of toilet stools, trough urinals, and a line of wash basins. I found it strange that the mirrors were made of steel and not of glass. After my father gave us a cook's tour of our new home, it became quite clear; there was no privacy.

Residing in the same hall as my brother and I were German merchant seamen. Some had been interned as early as April, 1941. I saw one particular seaman who was acting strangely, and I asked my father why he was like that. My father told us that he had become mentally ill, due to his long period of internment. He also told us to avoid him.

We awoke by the clock, ate by the clock, and went to bed by the clock. In other words, we were now on a very strict schedule. An unwritten code of the internees was that you kept your area clean—that is to say, you made your bed every morning, hung your towel neatly on the bed rack, dusted beneath your bed and maintained a well-kept area. The general and all-purpose areas were swept and mopped by the internees themselves. I even volunteered to swing the mop and mop the floors. Of course, I had to be instructed how to do it the correct way. I was a child on an island living with adult males.

At Ellis Island my formal education ceased. There were no classes for either my brother or me. I did however, receive good informal, skills training. During my first few days, I observed many internees who were craftsmen at work. I watched them make beautiful, detailed, highly polished jewelry cases in a variety of sizes from raw wood. I was most fascinated by the work of several of the internees who created scenes, like the Neuschwanstein Castle in Germany, using wood-burning tools. Several were scenes from the Bavarian Alps; others were of the Rhine River and its surroundings. The interned artisans were making "edelweiss" flowers from ivory or deer horn material, and others were building models of old ships, in and out of bottles. Most of the internees kept themselves busy from morning until night. If they were not doing their handcrafts, they were writing letters to their loved ones—their parents, their wives, their children or their sweethearts.

Many of the internees were prolific readers, and I too began to read more than ever before. My favorite books were westerns, and as I recall, most of what I read were stories that took place in the vicinity of the Pecos River in New Mexico. It became evident to me that keeping busy helped to pass the time on the island. It also helped me keep a sound mind.

Some of the men played checkers, while others played chess. Chinese checkers was also a popular board game. Some evenings full-length movies were shown. There were several Ping-Pong tables, and Ping-Pong was very popular among the internees. My father had become a decent player, and he taught my brother and me the game. It did not take long for us to become competitive.

My favorite pastime during my first month on the island was learning how to use the typewriter. First, I watched several internees type letters and other correspondence. Second, I had my father show me a few things about the typewriter. Third, I started my "hunt and peck" experience. The more I typed, the more familiar I became with the location of the keys. To this day, I have no recollection of what I typed or what I did with what I typed. It was a new experience for me, and I developed some good typing skills. When I became bored with typing, I tried my hand at crafts. Before we came to Ellis Island I had started making a billfold as part of a Boy Scout project. After I finished the billfold on the island, which was a so-so product, I began to make belts.

Belt making was appealing to me. Essentially, the belts were macramé. First I started with a simple belt, that was narrow, of a single color, and made with simple knots. As I became more experienced, I worked to see how quickly I could finish a complex belt with multi-colored cords and an assortment of knots in a variety of geometrical patterns. It was another way to pass away the time, while we waited, waited and waited for our turn to go to the family camp in Texas.

I do not know how my father and the other inmates managed to maintain their sanity on the island. Some men, including my father, walked in the compound for hours each day, but I did not find this appealing. Once in a while we would kick a soccer ball around the compound, but the walkers didn't appreciate this activity, because it interfered with their walking. The tempers of many internees were short, and it did not take much to set them off. There were turf arguments. Loud noises and running were not permitted.

Living on the island gave me a sense of being isolated from civilization. I lived in the shadow of Liberty—the Statue of Liberty—but had no liberty. I could see the skyline of New York City—but could not go there. I watched the ferry leave with people—taking them off of the island, but I could not leave. I could not escape. I observed the members of the U.S. Coast Guard leaving on a cutter, but I could not leave. These scenes made it even more ugly to be on the island. As the crow flies, Ellis Island was only about eight to ten miles in an easterly direction from the block where I lived in Brooklyn. So close, but yet so far away.

Sometimes I would stand by a window and stare at the waters in the harbor. I was fascinated by the whitecaps on top of the water. It was mesmerizing. Little did I know that my experience at Ellis Island prepared me for what I was to experience in the near future.

While we were at Ellis Island I do not believe that anyone wrote to us. I vaguely recall that my mother's cousin brought us cookies and visited my mother at the island. There were restrictions placed on the number of letters a person could send and receive. All mail was censored—read by others before it was mailed or received. I don't think that my friends had any idea as to our fate. One day we were there in our neighborhood, and the next day we were gone— we simply disappeared.

Chapter Nine

Going West—Crystal City, Texas

Finally the day, April 26, 1945, had arrived when we were to leave Ellis Island for Texas. Two Immigration and Naturalization Service or Border Patrol Agents, one male and one female, met us on the island and escorted us to the ferry. When we docked, the male agent handcuffed himself to my father and I was angry and embarrassed. Now the government was treating my father as if he were a criminal. The female agent made sure she remained in a very close proximity to my mother. As we made our way to the train station, the agents conversed with both of my parents; and once in a while, they would ask my brother and me questions. I thought they were trying to size us up.

When we boarded the train, the male agent spoke with the conductor, and showed him some papers. As soon as the train got underway, the agent took the handcuff off of my father's wrist. I remember the male guard saying to him, "I do not want to embarrass you or your family Mr. Jacobs, so I am going to let your family be together, and to dine as a family." After that the two agents remained in our railroad car, but they did not sit with us, or dine with us, and we had the "run" of the train. We appreciated the fact that they did not treat us as criminals. At stops, we had to return to our assigned seats. The three-day train ride to Uvalde, Texas, turned out to be a pleasant experience. One day during the trip we stopped in St. Louis, where we had a few hours layover. By then, our guards knew we were not going to flee, and they allowed my mother, my brother and me to leave the station, but they held my father inside. It was a beautiful day, and the first thing that came to my mind was the movie, *Meet Me in St. Louis*, starring Judy Garland. I remember saying to myself, "so this is St. Louis."

A day or so later we arrived at Uvalde where officials from the Crystal City Internment Camp[7] (Texas) of the Immigration and Naturalization Service met us. From there we were transported by bus to the internment camp which was forty miles south of Uvalde. For the next seven months our home would be in the Crystal City Family Internment Camp[8].

When we were inside the camp, I noticed that there was a large pole with streamers of many colors hanging from the pole. I asked my father about the significance of the pole and its streamers. He replied, "That's a Maypole and it is part of a May Day celebration, an old European custom." Then there was some processing and paperwork that took place. As we had at Ellis Island, we also had to use plastic "internment" money. My parents exchanged what little cash they had for this money, and once the processing was complete, we were taken to our "new" quarters.

We were quite disappointed and appalled when we first saw the living quarters. The duplex to which we were assigned had been shut up for a long time, and as we opened the door several wasps and other flying insects flew out in front of our faces. It smelled musty. The inside walls were unfinished;

---

[7] Crystal City, Texas is located approximately 120 mile southwest of San Antonio, Texas.

[8] The Crystal City Internment Camp was multicultural. Persons of German, Italian, and Japanese heritage were interned there. In addition, there were persons of German, Italian, and Japanese heritage from several Latin American republics. The camp was quasi segregated. The Japanese lived in one-half of the camp and the German and Italians in the other. Even though these ethnic groups were separated, they participated in many joint activities.

they were black, just like the outside tarpapered walls. There was neither a kitchen nor toilet facilities in the duplex. It had just two small rooms without any furniture except for four military-type beds. My father told my disappointed mother, "I will have this fixed up in no time." After we dropped off our bed linen, we were shown our assigned latrine and shower facilities, and our assigned mess hall. The latrine was smelly, and the urine troughs were filled with crickets, which were all over the place. I had already used public toilet and shower facilities at Ellis Island and thus the Crystal City public facilities were not a new experience, except for the crickets. At Ellis Island rats and roaches were common! As a matter of fact, the Crystal City shower and toilet facilities were much less crowded. I slowly became accustomed to the crickets hopping around in the urinal trough and on the shower floor, and to the musty smell of the facility.

My father had managed to find a type of "drywall" to put up on our walls and he purchased some paint. Soon our quarters would be brighter. My father painted the walls a light color and used a rag to put a rose-colored design on the walls. Mom made some curtains, began to gather some furniture, chairs and tables, and with each passing day our quarters became more livable and a place we could call home. Almost overnight my father and mother transformed a tarpaper shack to a pleasant set of rooms, and my mother was very pleased. In front of our duplex, my parents sowed morning glories and planted castor beans. Castor bean trees grew quickly in that part of Southwest Texas and it did not take long for us to have some shade in front of our duplex, just like the quarters of the more established internees. During that summer we also had beautiful morning glory vines growing in our own yard.

The next order of business for us was to schedule ourselves for medical and dental examinations. Then it came time to enroll in school, even though I was not looking forward to it. There were so many other things I could be doing besides going to school, like swimming, hiking, playing catch with my new friends, and even playing soccer. However, despite my sentiments about school, my parents enrolled my brother and me in school—the German School! At the time I did not know why we were enrolled in the German School, but later that year I would learn why.

I was registered in Klasse VI. When I left P.S. 81 in Brooklyn I was in the 7th Grade. Perhaps this Klasse VI was the German equivalent of the 7th Grade. Starting school was most difficult. Most of the students in my class had been in the camp for more than one school year, and their thoughts were different from mine. I also knew that most internees wondered about new inmates. Their unasked question was "I wonder why the Jacobs family was interned?"

My new classmates had already established their routine and friendships. I was the new kid on the block, and for a few days I found it most difficult to become accepted. I was, in a way, an obstacle to the others. I was an intruder. However, I kept trying and was able to befriend a Japanese American teenager, slightly older than I, and we flew kites together. As a matter of fact he taught me how to make a hexagon kite. I also went to a jujitsu class and to several sumu-wrestling matches with him. At the jujitsu class I met a Latin American German, who had been taking jujitsu classes for several months or longer and had been awarded a belt of some sort. In the next two or three months I made more friends. We not only played together but we watched basketball games between the Japanese and German internees. Often my Japanese American friend and I would eat together in the dining hall prescribed for those of us who did not have cooking facilities in our quarters. But our favorite pastime was swimming and diving at the camp pool. It was not an ordinary pool, but a vast circular water reservoir, approximately 150 feet in diameter, used for irrigation of the camp farm. Each morning about seven I would head for the pool, and usually, I was the first one there. During daylight hours, when I was not in school, I practically lived in that swimming pool.

The war ended in May, 1945. In June and July of that year, some of my new friends were released. My limited social group was in a constant state of flux. It got to the point that I avoided getting too friendly with many children of my generation because it was too risky. Many left without saying goodbye and often we did not know where they went.

School had its "exciting" days. During my first or second day of class, my German teacher observed that I was writing with my left hand. He remarked to me, "In this class you must write with your right hand." "What?" I said to myself. I could hardly wait until I got home to tell my father about this episode. When I arrived home, I told him what my teacher said about writing with my right hand. My father bristled for a moment, and then said, "Come on, let's go see your teacher." We walked to the school. When we met the teacher, my father introduced himself, and then said, "I understand you told my boy that he must write with his right hand." The teacher replied, "Ja."[9] My father then said, "My boy will write with whatever hand he chooses; this is America!" With that my father took me by the hand, and we turned around and went back home. This was the last of this incident, as I continued to write with my left hand, and my teacher said no more to me about it. The case was closed.

---

[9] Translated: Yes

My school subjects and respective grades consisted of:

Course	Grade
Writing German	Satisfactory
Speaking German	Satisfactory
English	Very Good
History	Good
Geography	Good
Nature	Good to Satisfactory
Arithmetic	Good
Geometry	Good
Physical Education	Good
Singing	Satisfactory
Drawing	Satisfactory to Unsatisfactory
Manual Arts	Satisfactory

I only went to school during the month of May, a few days in June; and from September 10, 1945 through November 26, 1945.

It was in November when I learned why my brother and I were enrolled in the German School—we were going to be expatriated to Germany. My father had volunteered to repatriate to Germany,[10] and my mother agreed to join him. Of course, as children, my brother and I had no choice in this matter. As it turned out my attendance in the German School would prove to be beneficial, even though I have no fond memories of my Crystal City class experiences like I do of P.S. 81 in Brooklyn.

---

[10] I have since learned that my father volunteered to be repatriated because the U.S. Department of Justice issued an order stating that he was to be deported. It is most doubtful whether this order was lawful because my father had two sons who were born in the United States and were citizens thereof.

My family did not dwell on internment at Crystal City, and as a matter of fact, there were times when I did not even think about internment. My community about me was ever changing, and there were fewer and fewer of us each day. In December of 1945, it was our turn to leave the camp. We were not freed, but taken with ninety-seven others to Ellis Island. Here my family and I would spend almost two more months, waiting for a ship to take us to Germany.

Author's additional notes about the Crystal City Family Internment Camp, Crystal City, Texas:

The Immigration and Naturalization Service with the aid of the U.S. Border Patrol and the Texas Board of Education operated the Crystal City Family Internment Camp. The camp was not a concentration camp, as it has been referred to by some. The officials, administrators, guards, and educators, of this camp treated the internees with human dignity. They attempted to provide the amenities of home as much as practical and possible, and in some instances they even stretched the rules to meet the health, welfare and morale needs of the internees. Most importantly they had great empathy for the mental and physical well being of their charges—the internees—and in particular the children. The officials of this camp served above and beyond the call of duty.

There were joint jujitsu classes, intramural basketball and baseball. There were cultural day exchanges and combined sports days. Many of the elder Germans were taking Japanese language classes as taught by one of the Japanese internees and vice-versa. The swimming pool was a common social gathering place for both the younger and older generations of Japanese Americans and German Americans. My father who worked both as a cook and baker in the dining hall worked side by side with persons of Japanese ancestry. Other German Americans and Japanese Americans also worked side by side.

Chapter Ten

The Isle of Tears—revisited

This story, about our trip from Crystal City back to Ellis Island, was told to me by R.C. Tate, Supervisor of Education, Crystal City Internment Camp. Tate was one of several men who was responsible for maintaining control over the 101 internees who left Crystal City on December 1, 1945 for Ellis Island, N.Y. Tate said that the plan was to exchange one of the passenger railroad cars when the train arrived in Cincinnati. This exchange was necessary because one of the railroad cars being used to transport internees was too tall to clear some of the tunnels between Cincinnati via Washington, D.C. to New York.

As we pulled into the Cincinnati station, Tate said he noticed a contingent of sharply dressed and armed U.S. Marines. He wondered why the troops were on the platform. When the train stopped, he got out of the train and asked the officer in charge of the Marines what was going on. The officer promptly reported that his contingent was there to guard the 101 dangerous Nazis on board the train. To which Tate promptly replied, "I do not need armed guards for this group of internees, and for your information they are not dangerous Nazis." The next person Tate had to confront was the stationmaster. The stationmaster advised him that one of the railroad cars had to be exchanged. Tate, asked, "While you exchange the car where are you going to put the passengers?" The stationmaster said, "Unload them and let them wait on the platform, while we exchange cars." Tate said, "Sir, it is freezing out there. Many of my passengers are women and children. They will not be able to tolerate such freezing conditions." To which the stationmaster replied, "Who cares, they are just a band of Nazis." Tate replied, "My passengers will not be unloaded on this platform while you exchange cars." The stationmaster explained to Tate that he was pressed for time and needed to exchange cars as quickly as possible. Tate told the stationmaster that he would move the passengers from the railroad car that had to be exchanged into the adjacent car with the other internees. The stationmaster did not like this idea because it would be time consuming. However, Tate stood firm, and we were spared from having to stand on the platform in sub-freezing weather while the railroad car was being exchanged.

When we arrived in New York, Tate was faced with a similar circumstance. The officials at the train station wanted him to unload his passengers and have them stand in the cold while they waited for bus transportation to arrive. Tate required that the transportation be available before "his" passengers debarked from the train. He demanded and received humane treatment for his charges. Like so many of the officials at Crystal City, Tate insisted that the internees be treated with respect and human dignity.

Some three or four days after we left Crystal City, we arrived back at Ellis Island. This time I was no longer a rookie on the island, and I knew my way around. I knew what to expect and I knew the ground rules. The procedures had not changed since I left in April earlier that year. There were some new faces, but many of the "old-timers" were still there.

Life on the island was much the same as before. The only notable changes were that overcrowded conditions were worse, and there were many comings and goings of Asian men. I believe they were Japanese. Several hundred or so men would arrive on the island each day. They would spend a day or two, then leave the island. This went on for days.

Presumably they were being shipped back to Japan. I was amazed at the large numbers that came and went.

As before, my brother and I were separated from our mother, and we, like my dad, were required to live in the open bay men's quarters just as we had earlier in the year. Because we were scheduled to go to Germany, we were required to have all of the appropriate inoculations. This started immediately, and I was sick for days after my first set of shots. My arm became so sore, that even the slightest movement was very painful. My arm felt as if it weighed a ton, and I was sick with pain.

I had no idea how long I would be there, so as before I began to find things to do. This time I spent less time making belts and more time reading western novels. Often I found myself just staring out of windows, and I dreamt of getting off the island. I also thought about my friends in the Brooklyn neighborhood. I would observe Coastguardsmen leaving the island on a Coast Guard cutter and I would imagine myself being on board the cutter with them in their sharp-looking uniforms. It was tough for me to watch them come and go, because once again I was playing the waiting game. I was waiting for our time to set sail for Germany.

Soon it was Christmas. A group of repatriates had left the island just a day or two before, but it was not our time. Christmas came and went. Then New Year's Day came and went. Our number finally came up on January 17, 1946. This day we were taken off the island aboard a U.S. Coast Guard Cutter. I was excited. Not excited to go to Germany, but to get off the island. The cutter delivered us to the S.S. Aiken Victory, and a member of the Aiken crew greeted us at the top of the gangplank, and another seaman showed us to our quarters. Shortly after we were aboard the ship and before the ship set sail, we were given fire drill and life jacket procedures. During the voyage, we had at least two

more such drills. For the next ten days the Aiken would be
our home.

.

Chapter Eleven

The Voyage

The crew of the Aiken were courteous and treated us with respect. They treated us as if we were first class passengers. In fact, I would say we received royal service. John Kincaid, a member of the crew, treated my brother and me as if we were his brothers. I have carried John Kincaid's name in my memory ever since this voyage.

I attribute my memorable impression of Kincaid (this is what he preferred to be called) to the fact that he was a warm, kind, and friendly person, and he told me that his hometown was Kincaid, West Virginia. Kincaid took the time to teach me how to walk when the ship rolled—for most of the voyage the Aiken was storm-tossed. However, there were moments of calm seas, and during these times, I recall standing in amazement on the ship's deck and watching the fish come up out of the water, as if they were flying and following the ship.

Many of the passengers became seasick, including my parents and my brother, but I was spared. Between meals, no matter the time of day, Kincaid would take me to one of the smaller galleys, a place where crewmembers drank coffee, shot the breeze and/or played cards. Sometimes I was allowed to join in when the seamen played rummy. Some played cribbage. Kincaid knew I had a sweet tooth, and he always managed to find some fine dessert for me. Once he personally escorted me from one end of the ship to the other, from stem to stern. Even the Chief Steward gave me a cook's tour of the galley and the pantry. Kincaid also gave me a tour of the troop quarters where the cots were stacked four high. He told me the Aiken was capable of carrying 1,500 soldiers.

During the entire voyage I don't believe I ever heard a cross or discouraging word from any crewmember towards their passengers, the repatriates. On the ship it was like heaven, but once we left the ship it was hell. There was no longer peace. There were no smiling faces, and there were no warm greetings. There was no friendliness. Like the weather, personal relationships were cold. We received no respect, and no one in charge cared about the treatment we were receiving.

From the time we left the ship's gangplank I only heard the constant shouting of orders. Some in English, but most in fractured German. I thought, why do they shout their orders in German? We spoke and understood English. Some of us, like myself, understood English better than we did German. I was confused. Why were American soldiers yelling at us? What did we do to deserve this? Who ordered this done to us? Why was it done?

In my cell I often wondered if the Aiken crew knew what was to befall us when we debarked. Had they transported other internees to Germany? Did they treat us this well because they knew of the handling that awaited us? Did they know that I would be transported in sub-freezing weather via truck and boxcar across Germany? Was this why one of the seaman gave my brother a warm wool-lined jacket? Did they know about a prison called Hohenasperg and the hangman's tree?

Chapter Twelve

Released, but not Free

I was released from Hohenasperg, as was my brother, on February 7, 1946. No explanations. No reasons for our release. No apologies for holding us in a place for high-ranking German officers suspected of war crimes. The officials simply gave us a train ticket from the town of Asperg to Ludwigsburg, where we were assigned to a minimum security internment camp.

The soldiers opened the inner gate of Hohenasperg prison, and we walked through it. As we passed through the inner gate, it was closed behind us, and we were inside a tunnel. Then we walked though this short tunnel and when we reached the outer gate, it was opened. Finally, I was out of this place, and I never looked back. My brother and I walked down the hill into the village of Asperg, and went to the train station where we got on the train to Ludwigsburg. Once we arrived, we reported to the assigned camp.

In this camp we had no extraordinary restrictions placed on us. Just the usual, off the streets at or before dark and any other martial law rules implemented by the United States Army for the American Zone of occupied Germany. And, we had to remain in the vicinity until my father was released. We were fed on the street at about dusk. Several ladies from the Red Cross would come to an intersection with what appeared to be five-gallon thermoses. Those to be fed, and there were many, would line up, one behind the other. Nothing was served until the line was orderly. Once the line was orderly the women of the German Red Cross would begin to serve. Each person received one bowl of soup. The soup was mostly water flavored by bouillon, which had very little nutritional content. There were no second helpings, and I always left the "supper table" hungry. There was no lunch meal, and at breakfast we received one glass of "gray" milk and one slice of black bread. I always had hunger pangs while we were in that camp. Nevertheless, I was thankful for the morsels of food we received. It was better than the bread and water I received during the ninety-two hour ride in the boxcar and the conditions under which I ate these morsels were a thousand times better than the situation at Hohenasperg.

During most of my childhood it was my nature to explore. I liked to visit different places. Before I was twelve I had traveled the subway and elevated trains of New York alone from one end of the line to the other. I only got lost once; I was out of money, and I was standing at a trolley stop crying, when a trolley car operator picked me up and drove me home in his trolley. Thus, after I was released from prison, I naturally began to explore Ludwigsburg and its surrounding area.

My explorations of the area began when I hitchhiked with my brother to Stuttgart. When we first got there, I noticed the U.S. Mounted Constabulary. They were sharp looking troops, and wore white silk-like scarves and chrome-plated helmets as they patrolled the streets in their vehicles. Their vehicles had the shape of a tank, but were on rubber tires. A machine gun mounted on a circular track was at the top center of the vehicle, which allowed the gunner to aim the machine gun in any direction. These men and their vehicles were visible throughout the city.

If too many people gathered anywhere, the constabulary would break them up. Persons so gathered were instructed to move on. One day while we were in Ludwigsburg the constabulary instructed all males, irrespective of age, to go to a local theater. We were literally rounded up. It was like a

63

dragnet, and the constabulary in both their tank-like vehicles and on their motorcycles gathered all the men and boys they could find and directed them to the theater. As we approached the theater other members of the constabulary would instruct us to go inside. I had no idea what was going on. After the theater was filled, an armed constabulary appeared on the stage at the front of the theater. His instructions were that we were to watch a movie. We were not to close our eyes or to turn our heads away from the screen. This was the first time I had ever been forced to go to a movie. I could not imagine the purpose of what was happening. Then the lights were dimmed. In the aisles were several members of the constabulary pacing up and down and looking from side to side. At the rear of the theater there were members of the constabulary guarding the exit doors. There was no way out.

Then the motion picture began. What we were being forced to watch was unedited, unexpurgated, raw, and crude military films of the concentration and death camps, the mass graves sites, the furnaces, the showers, the faces of the emaciated starving prisoners, and the faces of death. Both my brother and I became sick. Why was I forced to sit and watch these movies? I was an American. I had nothing to do with these war crimes. I was just a child. Was someone trying to send me a message? If so, what was the message?

Even to this day, when photos or films of the Holocaust are shown I have flashbacks to the day I was rounded up, forced to go into the theater, then forced to watch films of horror, films of man's inhumanity to man. I was only thirteen. I was an American who had worked daily to help the war effort of the United States of America, and this was my reward.

My second close encounter with the constabulary occurred one evening when my brother and I inadvertently violated curfew. We had gone to Stuttgart and did not get back to Ludwigsburg before dark. We knew we were violating the curfew, and when we arrived in Ludwigsburg we used as many side streets as possible to get to our barrack.

Out of nowhere came the roar of an armored constabulary patrol vehicle. We had been spotted. From a distance they flashed their spotlights in our direction. I told my brother, "Let's run for it! Head for the tracks." We both ran as fast as we could. First we jumped up on a three-foot wall, then ran up the railroad track embankment. On the way up the embankment, I kept slipping and falling on the gravel. My brother yelled, "Hurry up! They're getting closer." When I was almost half way up the slope, the constabulary shined their spotlight right on us. I thought they had a bead on one or both of us, and I was waiting for the 50-caliber machine gun to fire, but it didn't happen. Once we were over the top we went down the other side and fell to the ground. I could hear the roar of the engine as they continued to search and patrol up and down the street. Finally, they left the area. Then we got up and started back to our quarters.

We had achieved our mission, and the constabulary did their duty—they scared the living daylights out of us. After this incident, needless to say, we were never out after curfew. A short time after this incident my father was released from Hohenasperg.

Chapter Thirteen

A *New* Country—A *New* Culture

In the middle of March, 1946 my family was once again together. Just after my father was released from Hohenasperg, my mother was released from Camp 77, another Seventh Army internment camp, and my brother and I were released from the camp in Ludwigsburg. I believe my brother and I had been in the same camp as my mother, but in a different barrack.

After we got together, we boarded a train, and headed north for Bremen. This train, unlike the train that brought us here, was an unguarded civilian passenger train. We had papers that permitted us to leave the American zone and enter the British Zone where my grandparents lived. I think we had to change trains once or twice, but I do not recall when or where. When we boarded the train, the first thing I asked my father was, "Why didn't the Americans bring us down on a train like this?" My father simply shrugged his shoulders. To say the least this ride was different than the one that brought us to Ludwigsburg. Along the way I saw destruction: destroyed tanks, trucks, bridges, cities and train stations—massive devastation and carnage.

When we arrived at the Hauptbahnhof Bremen,[11] the main train station in Bremen, I could not believe my eyes. All of the glass within and without the station had been broken, and everything was blackened. I remember walking outside and seeing nothing but destruction in all directions. No one was

---

[11] Bremen was an enclave stipulated as an American Occupation Zone. Entry and egress restrictions were not as demanding as it was between other areas and occupation zones.

inside the station to greet us. We carried our suitcases to the front of the station and finally my father's sister's husband, my uncle by marriage, waved at us from his small car. The greeting was cold, and my uncle was somewhat put out. I could tell that he was not happy to be there to pick us up, and he had very little to say to any of us. Somehow we all managed to squeeze into his car, luggage and all.

From the Bremen train station to where my grandparents lived in Stickgras by Delmenhorst in the British Occupation Zone was about a twenty mile drive. Once we left the city of Bremen visually speaking, it was not as evident that a war had taken place. The only noticeable evidence was that there were bunkers to which the people had gone during air raids. These rural area bunkers were single-story, long, black buildings with entrances at both ends. The road we traveled was made of black, square cobblestones.

When we arrived at the home of my grandparents we entered through a gateway that was in the front of the house. One of the posts upon which a gate was supposed to be hinged had been damaged—knocked down. From the gate to the front steps of the home was about 150 feet. My grandmother, grandfather, an aunt and her son were on the front steps to greet us.

For the most part it was a cold greeting on a warm spring day. My grandmother gave me what I would call a formal hug. Her hug was not of love, but of obligation. My grandfather, on the other hand, was quite warm, cordial, and most interested in who I was and what I was made of. I could tell that there was a warm place in his heart for me. A long period of time passed before we were invited into the home. My aunt, uncle and their son lived in the same house, as did my grandparents. Their living quarters were on the second story and included kitchen facilities. We lived downstairs with my grandparents.

67

It was clear that relationships were strained. We were "strangers," intruders and worst of all we, my brother and I, were Americans, the victors. This did not set too well with some of the Germans with whom I came in contact. In addition, we were four more persons to feed. Germany was war-torn and starving, and there was little to eat. Food items were rationed. Each person of school or working age was required to have a card, and this card had to be stamped each month by an official of the occupying government, reflecting that you were either working or in school. If it was not stamped you didn't receive your rations of milk and bread.

My father, brother, and I helped my grandfather, Opa, transform his lawns into gardens. My father removed the sod, and Opa, my brother and I turned the soil with a spade, and then we planted potatoes. Subsequently, we re-dug and enlarged an underground shelter in which we could store our food crops to keep the vegetables and fruit we stored from freezing. In this area the soil often froze to a depth of eighteen inches.

Opa also acquired some rabbits. It was my job to go out along the roadsides each morning to gather dandelions for the rabbits. This was a competitive business, because many others were also gathering dandelions. The youngest dandelion weeds would be gathered for salads and if you found more mature ones, those would be used to feed the rabbits. Once or twice a month Opa would slaughter a rabbit for us to eat, and we used the hides to line our wooden shoes. Like the Dutch, we wore wooden shoes when we worked in the garden or went out to chop or get firewood. Coal, like our food, was rationed.

Each month my brother and I would take my Opa's wagon and go to the coal yard to purchase our ration of briquettes. The coal was shaped in the form of a brick but was a bit smaller. One time when we were coming back from the coal yard, a man tried to steal our coal. We were able to keep him from getting the coal, because I started running with the wagon behind me, and my brother kept fending off the man.[12] We never gave up a briquette of coal.

Our dress, mannerisms, and appearance gave us away as foreigners. After awhile in our neighborhood we became known as the "Amis," short for Americans. This was particularly noticeable in the school we attended for a short period. Both my brother and I attended the local school, but we found it to be difficult. Everything was taught in German and it was our job to understand the subject and be able to pass a test on the material covered in class. Due to our limited German it was tough, to say the least. Within a couple of months I told my father I did not want to go to school anymore. He reluctantly agreed, but reminded me that the alternative was that I had to work.

However, finding work was not that easy. I walked to the Labor Office in the town of Delmenhorst, which was two to three miles from our home. The office was operated by the British Army, but was predominantly staffed with German nationals.

When I arrived I asked a soldier for directions and he pointed to a desk. I walked over to the desk, and the German official behind the desk asked me in German, "And, what do you

---

[12] Syker Strasse is the name of the street on which the coal yard was located. It was two or three miles from where we lived. The street was lined with huge oak trees, trees which I was told were planted in the days of Napoleon. The Winter of 1946/1947 was one of the coldest winters on record in Germany. Despite this, and the shortage of heating fuels, it was against the law for persons to use any part of these oak trees for firewood. Oddly, these trees were cut down sometime in the 1970s to widen the road.

want?" I told him that I wanted a work card. At this point he started to lecture me that I should be in school and not working. In my broken German mixed with English, I told him I had discussed this with my father, and my father had agreed that I could quit school and go to work. I received another lecture from the German official behind the desk, and then he asked me, "What is your nationality?" I replied, "American." His face got fiery red, and again, in German, he said, "You are not an American!" I replied, "I am too!" This irritated him more. Then he told me to speak German. I told him I had some difficulty speaking German and preferred speaking English. I spoke in English to try to prove to him that I was an American. The more I spoke in English, the more annoyed he became. He gave me a form to complete, but the entire form was written in German. I did not understand several of the questions, and I asked him for help. This made him even madder. I sensed that I was digging a hole for myself.

I had my own ideas as to what Nazis were like in Germany, and this man seemed to fit my model. After a long harangue and argument with him, he handed me my Arbeitskarte[13]. Once I had the card in my hand, I took one step backward, clicked my heels together, promptly raised my right arm and gave the Nazi salute, and said, "Sieg Heil!" He came over the top of the desk and started to chase me, but I outran him. I hoped that I would never have to go back to that office again.

After this incident I had great empathy for my father. I now understood what he went through to get his job. The German officials who were working for the British placed my father in one of the lowliest jobs available. He was assigned to work in the peat fields, which was back breaking

---

[13] Translated: Work Card

work. My father had to ride a bike several miles to and from work, and when he arrived home he would be completely exhausted.

Peat was the most commonly available fuel after the war. All day long my father and the other laborers would cut bricks of peat. Then they would stack them, and when they were dried they would be taken to the market for sale, where each purchase was limited to the rationed amount. One day when my father came home from work, he collapsed as he came into the house. Emergency personnel were called, and they lifted my father into his bed. Then they announced he was paralyzed, but fortunately, the paralysis was temporary. This forced my father to seek new employment, and eventually he was employed by the United States Army.

Chapter Fourteen

Angels

After I had my work card I began to explore my surroundings. Just over a mile north of where I was living there was a major highway named Bremer Strasse. Traveling east on this highway led to Bremen, an American enclave in the British Occupation Zone. Going west on this highway led to Delmenhorst and Oldenburg, both in the British Occupation Zone. I walked down to this highway many times, and sat and watched the cars and trucks going by. During these periods; I noticed that many British Army vehicles also traveled this highway, but very few U.S. vehicles did. However, at about ten o'clock each morning an American weapons carrier would come by heading west. I made a mental note of this.

One morning, as usual, I strolled down to Bremer Strasse, and sure enough, at about ten o'clock in the morning a U.S. 3/4-ton Weapons Carrier was headed west, in my direction. Just a few feet before the vehicle got to me, I held out my thumb and hand in hitchhiking fashion. Just as the truck passed by, the driver slammed on the brakes, and geared down quickly. Then the driver put the weapons carrier in reverse and backed up until I was next to the passenger door.

The soldier looked at me and said, "Where are you going?" I replied, "Delmenhorst." He said, "Get in." I got in the front passenger seat. Before he proceeded to drive the truck, he asked, "When did you learn the American way of hitchhiking?" I said, "I am an American?" He said, "What, you're an American? What are you doing here?" I proceeded to tell him the story of how my father was arrested, interned, and repatriated. I told him why my mother, brother and I had to go along. Then, the soldier told me his name was "Endicott."

Endicott was both surprised and suspicious to learn about what happened to me. He told me he had another former internee with him that he would like for me to meet. He turned to the rear of his covered weapons carrier and said, "Johnny, I want you to meet an American who was interned in the United States." Johnny popped his head through the canvas, and said in somewhat fractured English, "Hi, I'm Johnny the Czech." I then introduced myself to him and told him that I was glad to meet him.

After the introduction was over, Endicott told me that Johnny the Czech had been in Buchenwald or Auschwitz, two German concentration camps. Then he turned to Johnny once more, and said, "Johnny, show him your tattoo." Johnny turned his arm over and on the inside of his forearm there were some numbers. I asked Johnny, "Where are your parents?" He replied, "I don't know." I felt uneasy about asking him more about his family and dropped the subject. The weapons carrier proceeded down the road, with me in the front seat. I did not know why Johnny the Czech was riding in the back, but I guessed it was because of the travel restrictions placed on us.

While we were driving, Endicott asked me, "Why are you going to Delmenhorst?" I told him I was looking for a job. He then stated, "Maybe you can work for the United States Army in Oldenburg, in Graves Registration." I asked, "What would I do?" He replied, "Don't worry about that. We will find something for you to do." Oldenburg, was approximately 30 miles or so from my home, and I wondered how I could get to and from work. In the meantime, Endicott asked me many questions as to where I was born in the United States and where I lived. He even asked me to name my favorite baseball team. I responded, "The

73

Brooklyn Dodgers." He asked me one question after another. I sensed all during the questioning period that Endicott was wondering whether I was actually an American. Once he was satisfied that I was an American, his questioning ceased. I had experienced many others, Americans, British and Germans, who doubted my veracity, so I was not a rookie to his line of questioning.

When we arrived in Oldenburg, Endicott stopped at a private home that had been appropriated by the military for living quarters for the U.S. Occupation forces. This is where he was quartered. Endicott, Johnny the Czech, and I went into the house. He introduced me to all of his buddies. After he had finished introducing Johnny and me, he asked us to unload the back of the weapons carrier. There were sundry items, canned goods, rations, toilet paper, and soap powders on board.

After Johnny and I unloaded the truck, Endicott drove me to the United States Army Forces Graves Registration Headquarters. It was in a military post a mile or two from the house, where we had dropped off the groceries. When we got there we refueled the truck, parked it, and then went into the administrative office. Endicott asked an officer in the office if they could employ me. He went on to say, "This boy is an American, or at least he claims he is." I guess he still had doubts. I was then asked to fill out a form for employment. When I finished it, I was asked, "Do you understand German? Do you speak German?" I told both of them that my handle on the German language was good enough to get around. Then simultaneously they asked, "Where did you learn German?" That took some explaining. I went through the routine of the Crystal City German School, and told them how my mother taught me a few words at home. That seemed to satisfy both of them. "You are hired," the officer said. He said, "You will be our interpreter. You can talk to the Burgermeisters[14] when we need to do some work in the rural villages."

I said, "I live in Stickgras by Delmenhorst. How will I get to and from work?" The officer replied, "We will find quarters here for you. And on weekends or whenever we make a commissary and PX run to Bremen, someone can stop by your home so you can visit your parents and pick up your stuff." That same day I met Woods, another GI who worked with Endicott. They drove me home and met my parents. My parents were excited, because they had not spoken to Americans, since they had been in Germany. My mother made "ersatz," which was a poor substitute for coffee. As Endicott and Woods sipped their ersatz, Endicott turned to my mother and said, "You need real coffee." He got up from the table and said he would be right back. He went down to the truck and brought up a bag of groceries, including canned milk, candy bars, coffee, and American brand washing powders. I was as surprised as my parents that Endicott had brought goods with him. I had not asked him for anything. It was obvious he knew what the shortages were, and he knew that the people of Germany were on a starvation diet. This event was the beginning of a warm relationship between my parents and the GIs for whom I would be working. Endicott, like John Kincaid, treated me as if I was his little brother. I was delighted to have such a wonderful new friend. I do believe that Endicott sincerely believed that I was an American, but remained reluctant in public to make this assertion. Generally when he introduced me to his friends he would start by saying, "This boy says he is an American…"

My citizenship identity was quite a struggle for me. I was proud to be an American, and I didn't like people to call me

---

[14] Translated: Mayors

a German. Sometimes it would even make me hostile towards them. I knew I was an American, I simply had no proof. I needed proof. I had no idea how to establish that proof, but I thought about it a lot. My country sent me to this land without papers. Why did they do that? How did they make me leave without a passport? These questions nagged at me. Sometimes even the local Germans accused me of being an imposter. I was not!

It was during my employment with the Army Graves Registration that I learned more about the carnage and devastation of war. My work took me not only to countryside villages, but to major cities as well. I went to Essen, Cologne, Aachen, Koblenz, Frankfurt, Mainz, and Mannheim and to many points in between. Each day I would see rubble, rubble and more rubble. Many of the cities I visited were completely flattened. In many of the cities the only visible structures were the steeples of churches. In the rural areas burned out tanks, and destroyed trucks and jeeps decorated the countryside. Sometimes when we would drive through bombed out cities, I would reflect back on when we first arrived in Germany and I viewed the carnage in Bremen; it was almost too much for my young mind to bear. Detours were more common than direct highway routes. Bridges were either out or unsafe for crossing. Sometimes we would travel on unchartered highways and byways. Many of the roads had detours, and many times during our travels a detour sign would appear without warning. On several trips I was quite frightened and so was the driver. My most memorable trip was when the fog was so dense we had to drive slow enough to allow me to walk each step of the way in front of the jeep to make sure there was a road ahead.

During the entire time I worked for the Graves Registration, Endicott, Woods, and others would periodically drop into my parents' home and pay them a visit. The GIs provided them with sorely needed food. Often they would give my parents a report on me. They would make these stops on their way to or from their supply and mail runs to Bremen. Each time I would return home for a weekend, my mother would tell me that Endicott and Woods came by this week and dropped off some more groceries for us. Then Mom would go on to explain how she and my father shared these groceries with a refugee and his wife, and two more needy families in our neighborhood. I was always gratified to learn that my parents shared what little they had with others who had even less.

Each time Endicott and Woods stopped by, my mother said, "Endicott was full of questions." She always complimented both of them, telling me they were such fine young men. Endicott would begin by asking my mother, "Mrs. Jacobs, tell me more about the circumstances that brought you back to Germany." My mother would tell them of our trek. Endicott, Mom said, just could not understand how this could happen in the States—the United States of America. On one of the later visits my mother described our trip in the boxcar and told Endicott and Woods how her two sons were taken to Hohenasperg. "Both of them almost fell out of their chairs," Mom said. That next week when Endicott picked me up at my house he told me what my mother said and he wanted to know if all this actually happened. That is to say, was I really locked up in Hohenasperg and did an American soldier threaten to hang me if I was not a good boy. I told him it was the absolute truth. Then he found a place to pull over on the side of the road and stopped. He said, "Before we go any further I have a lot of questions for you. Tell me more about Hohenasperg."

I explained to Endicott that Hohenasperg and the boxcar were my nightmares. I described the events, which at this time remained vivid. I told him about the soldiers calling me a "little Nazi." I explained how from the time we left the ship in Bremerhaven until I arrived in my cell, soldiers were constantly shouting and yelling orders at us, sometimes in English and at other times in fractured German. It was frightening, I said. I tried to illustrate to him how I was required to walk when I was outside of my cell. I told him how frightened I was each time I passed the hangman's tree. I even told him, sometimes I thought that the hangman's tree was just in a dream I had, and was not real. "I know it sounds like a horror story," I told him, "but it's the truth."

Endicott then questioned me more about my childhood, "What schools did you attend? What grade were you in when you left school? What was your teacher's name? What street did you live on? Did you live in a house? Where were you born?" He fired off one question after the other. He even asked me about baseball players and baseball teams besides the Brooklyn Dodgers. He asked "all" of his questions before I could even answer the first question. I sensed that he was quite frustrated. I think he still had doubts that I was who I said I was. He was unsure of where I came from, and how I got to Germany. I also believe that sometimes he thought he had been had, and that it was a hoax, so that I could get food and work. I think Endicott was unsure because he did not want to believe that American GIs had treated my family and me as they did. He did not want to accept what my mother and I told him as the truth. After several hours of discussion and questioning Endicott sat back, "I just cannot believe what I am hearing." He asked, "Are you sure that you are telling me the truth?" I replied, "Yes, sir." Then I would think about something unique that I could say that would remove all doubt from Endicott's mind. I talked about how I traded baseball cards with my friends. I described how we flipped for baseball cards, and even told him about stoopball. I thought he would be familiar with this game, but he didn't have a clue. I told him about the subways and elevated trains in Brooklyn. I described the difference between the BMT and IRT subway lines, and that it took another coin to transfer between the two. I described Times Square, Central Park, Fifth Avenue, Park Avenue, Coney Island and Steeplechase Park for him. Finally I think I convinced Endicott once and for all that I was an American citizen. From then on he asked me no more questions about my past.

We sat along the road for awhile and Endicott seemed to be thinking. He then told me that we needed to figure out how to get me an American passport. He said, "You need proof to show others that you are in fact an American citizen. The next time I drive into Bremen I will take you to the American Consulate."

Unfortunately, there was not to be a next time. A few days after Endicott's roadside chat, sometime in the Fall of 1946, a new commander took over the Army Graves Registration Detachment in Oldenburg. Along with this command change the detachment was beginning to phase out and/or was being combined with other units in Germany. The new commander advised me that I would no longer be able to occupy a bunk in the GI barrack. He said it was against Army regulations. This ended my job with the U.S. Army. I was disappointed but I had learned many things, not the least of which was the ability to drive a variety of vehicles before my fourteenth birthday—jeeps, weapons carriers, and 2.5 ton 6x6 trucks. I knew I would be losing yet another set of friends. Friends who made sure that I had the proper clothing, proper food, and that my mother and father also received sufficient rations. Friends who cared for me like a brother. Sure enough, after this change I did not hear from Endicott or Woods again. Whatever changed, it surely happened on short notice. I knew they would not have abandoned my family or me. They were either rotated back to the States or shipped to another country. Another pair of friends, lost without a trace.

During the period I worked for the Graves Registration my parents had taken in Flüchtlinger[15] from the east. There was one man I named Paul Bunyan because of his stature. He and his petite and frail wife (both were a bit older than my parents) had no place to live. He worked with my father in the peat fields. My father told us that he often shared part of his lunch sandwich (mostly tomato sandwiches) with Bunyan. He observed that Bunyan would eat only one-half of what he gave him, and would wrap the other half in a rag and stick it in his coat. Later my father learned that Bunyan gave the half he saved to his wife, when he arrived home in the evening. He and his wife had been living in the woods or wherever they could find shelter, and the food they ate came from the land. During the day, Bunyan's wife would go through the woods and gather loose bits of wood and bark. Then she would take the sack of material collected and go house to house to exchange her findings for food.

When my father learned of this, he invited the Flüchtlinger to live with him and Mom. They were practically starved when my mother and father took them in. All the foodstuffs that my mother and father had been receiving from the American GIs were shared with their new refugee friends. I was proud that my parents had taken in the refugees. Neither the ordeal my father went through before returning to Germany nor his return had changed my father's good heartedness and his willingness to share with others as he did in Brooklyn. Many have said of my father that he would give you the shirt off his back.

---

[15] Translated: Refugees

Chapter Fifteen

The Winter of 1946/1947

The Winter of 1946/1947 and our own situation reminded my father of another winter, the Winter of 1917/1918. He told me that he had eaten turnips, a food normally fed to livestock, particularly pigs, for three meals a day. It was all they had. They had turnips for breakfast in the form of fried like potato cakes; at lunch they had diced turnips, and for supper mashed turnips.

Like the winter of 1917/1918, we knew the winter 1946/1947 as the Kohlrube Winter—the turnip winter. We too had turnips morning, noon, and night—this was our diet. The people of Germany were starving, and there was hardly any food or fuel available to the cities. Fortunately, we lived in the country, and if we could keep the rabbits from freezing to death and find some food to feed them, we could have a rabbit once in awhile. Hunger, malnutrition, freezing to death, disease, and the danger of epidemics were all part of daily "life" throughout Germany. I was out of work. Rations were reduced. The calorie allowance in the British Occupation Zone was down to 1,014 calories per person. In mid-1946 the weight of the average adult male in the U.S. Occupation Zone was 51 kilograms, or 112 pounds. By November of 1946, the food supply situation had reached a stage of collapse; and during this winter, fuel availability shrunk even more. Child mortality in one city, Mannheim, had reached 18 per 100. In 1936 it was only 6 per 100. In the cities of the U.S. Occupation Zone 26 percent of all deaths were children. By December of 1946 and January 1947 industrial production sank by 85 percent. Food shortages had reached such great proportions that in the Ruhr region of Germany demonstrations and riots broke out.

I lived through this starvation period—the winter of 1946/1947. I was out of work, and our food supply line through the GIs of the Graves Registration had dried up. The GIs we knew had either transferred to other parts of Germany or were rotated back to the United States. Personally, I had become desperate. I began to sneak into the U.S. Enclave in Bremen. I say "sneak" because during my entire stay in Germany we were under travel restrictions. To leave your assigned zone of occupation, one needed permission, and I had none. The automobile bridge was out, but there was a catwalk footbridge across the Weser River. I had to hitchhike to Bremen, and I would try to get to this footbridge during the early morning rush hour. I did this because at this time the sentry at the entry to the footbridge rarely closely examined the papers of those who used this catwalk. So I would mix in with several people who had official papers and wave my card as they did. I made many, many crossings in and out of Bremen and was not caught a single time. My strategy was that if I were caught, I would say, I forgot to bring my temporary pass, and I will go home and get it. I never had to use this excuse. The very first time I crossed the footbridge I was somewhat frightened that I would be caught and I was a bit timid once I was on the swaying footbridge. Constantly in the back of my mind was the fact that before nightfall I would have to return on the same footbridge. Would the sentry on the east side of the bridge be as lax as the west side sentry? If I were caught I intended to use the same excuse, "I must have forgotten my temporary pass."

Routinely I made this crossing, and some weeks I went every day. While in Bremen I attempted to make contact with Americans. When I became cold or tired I went into the American Red Cross River Club. This was a club where American soldiers could play pool, buy milkshakes, cigarettes and candy bars. However, I had no military scrip, and thus, I could not buy anything. I could only dream. Some soldiers would come in and play the piano to which I would listen for hours. At the same time, I would observe other GIs playing pool and billiards. It was warm inside the club. Winter had begun to set in and outside it was for the most part zero or sub-zero weather. It wasn't always easy to get into the club, particularly when there was an attendant at the door checking for military identification. Even under these conditions I would try to get in by saying I was looking for a friend. Sometimes I got in, but most of the time I did not.

My search for work, food, and friendship with Americans went on for weeks. My successes were intermittent. I met some U.S. Merchant Marines, but I have not been able to recall their names. I only recall that one of the seamen's fathers lived in Louisiana. This seaman gave me his father's address, and told me that if I returned to the United States and needed a place to live, I should contact his father. The seaman knew that I had tried to gain access to more than one American ship in the Port of Bremen. If I got on board I intended to stow away until I was in a United States port. There I would declare my citizenship and once again be a free person in the land I loved.

Several of the merchant seamen I met during this winter knew that I wanted to return to the United States. Each of them advised me that if I got by the guard at the entry of the ship, that is to say the person who was checking credentials at the top of the gangplank, they would assist me once I was on board.

We, the seamen and myself, developed a plan. The plan was that as they approached their ship sometime before midnight, they would start singing and acting as if they were drunk. I would be in their midst. Then as they started walking up the gangplank the seamen would become more boisterous. It was hoped that the ship's sentry would be lax, and would let each of them pass after he identified the first seaman. It was not to be. Twice we tried this, but on both occasions the sentry on duty at the top of the gangplank stopped me from boarding the vessel. I was caught because I was only thirteen and much too young looking to be a merchant seaman. Then came the scary part of my venture. I had to walk back alone through the pitch-black port and its surrounding area. There was always the possibility of being mugged, but it would be worse to be caught and arrested by the U.S. Navy Shore Patrol, because traveling, without official authority, outside of the Occupation Zone of my residence could result in a jail sentence.

Fortunately for me, during my second stowaway attempt a different sentry was on duty, because the first time I tried this the sentry on duty told me, as did the second, "Don't try to gain access to a U.S. merchant ship again, and stay out of the port area." After the second failure, and not wanting to press my luck, I gave up on the idea of stowing away to get back into the United States.

At every turn I had been thwarted. I could not find work, and my attempts to stowaway had failed. Friendships were few and far between. I had even become skeptical about developing new friends because they were here today and gone tomorrow. Relationships ended abruptly. What am I doing here? What brought me here? Why won't people believe that I am an American? If I only looked older, I thought, I would have no problem passing for a soldier.

As time went on, I became more depressed and frustrated. However, I continued going into Bremen, the U.S. Enclave, for the purpose of making contact with Americans. Day after day I went without a successful contact, and I had to stand outside in the cold. I hung around the American Red Cross Club, but my ability to gain access diminished. I had been caught so many times, I think the club management was always on the lookout for me, and that the staff was directed to keep me out. Now it was up to me to make contact with American GIs on the street before they entered the club. In a fashion, I became a beggar, except that I was not begging for money or for food, but for a job. One day while standing there, the outside temperature dropped rapidly. Both my ears and my feet began to freeze. It got to the point that I could not wiggle my toes. My feet ached, and I was becoming desperate. I did not think I could make it back to my home unless I found a warm spot. I could hardly walk. I could stand my frozen ears, but my feet were really hurting. My body was also becoming numb. In order to generate some warmth, I clicked my feet together and swayed back and forth. This did little, if any, good.

My last hope was to try to gain access to the American Movie Theater, a short block or two from the American Red Cross Club. Each step of the way my feet ached more severely. I had hoped when I was in front of the theater I could get someone to buy me a ticket. In order to purchase a ticket one had to have an identification card that identified oneself as a member of the U.S. military or as a U.S. civilian. This cold day there were few theatergoers. As a prospective patron walked by I would quietly ask, "Would you buy me a ticket?" None offered to do so. Most passerbys simply shrugged their shoulders and kept walking up to the cashier's window, leaving me out in the cold. As time went on I got colder and colder. My feet ached more and more. I did not think that I could take another step. At this point I was so **depressed and so cold that I was ready to give up on life. I had serious thoughts about just lying down and going to** sleep on the street. Instead, I finally wised up and headed for home. By the time I got home both of my ears had been frostbitten. My feet remained numb, but were not damaged.

After this experience I learned my lesson. I was not going to roam the streets of Bremen in mid-winter again. The remainder of that winter I just stayed home. In early March, the cold weather finally subsided. I needed to find work; so off to Bremen I went. As usual I went across the catwalk without a hitch with the workers. On one of my visits to Bremen, I located a large U.S. Army headquarters building. It was a large rectangular multistory structure, and the outside of the building was off-white in color. This building consisted of barrack-type living quarters for American soldiers, and it was also the headquarters for the U.S. Army Provost Marshal's office. At the time I went into the building I had no idea it included both offices and living quarters. I thought it was just a barrack.

There was no security around or in the building. However, the notice on the entry door read **"Authorized Military Personnel Only."** I had grown accustomed to these types of signs and like most people, I ignored them. After I went into the building I headed for the GIs' living quarters—the barrack portion of the building. I was looking for work. Several soldiers were in the barrack, some fully dressed, some in their shorts, and others still in their beds. As I walked through the barrack I offered to polish the shoes for the soldiers who were up and about. One after the other they turned me down. Then about midway through the barrack a soldier stopped me and said, "How come you speak such good English." I replied, with my usual story. I told the soldier I was an American. That would lead to another question. If you are an American, what are you doing in Germany? I would then tell my story. I would also note that I was always in search of a way back to the United States. Then it happened.

A soldier, who had been listening to me, said he doubted my story. He was sitting up, half-dressed in his bed. I had noticed that after he questioned the truthfulness of my story, he attempted to light his cigarette with a cigarette lighter. He kept flicking at the flint wheel but the lighter did not flame. After he had tried several more times, I said to the soldier, "You need 'benzene' for your lighter." He went into a rage. He yelled, "You're not an American, you're a Kraut." I was quite embarrassed. Several of the soldiers, who had been sleeping, rose up in their beds and asked, "What is going on here?" The outraged soldier went on to say, "I caught you, you little Kraut, didn't I? You gave yourself away when you used the word 'benzene.' I knew you'd slip up." "Benzene," he said, "is a Kraut term for gasoline and lighter fluid." I tried to get a word or two in, but he would not let me talk. He went on and on about how I had slipped up and that he had caught me. When I finally got a word in, I said, "'Benzene' is an English word, it's in the dictionary. Get me a dictionary," I said, "and I will show you." He would not listen, and continued to rant and rave. Then he shouted, "Get out of this barrack!" As I started to turn away from him he told me to stop. He told me he was going to take me to the Provost Marshal's office. He said, "You are an imposter." By now, I thought I had done myself in. Here I was in the American Enclave, and I lived in the British Occupation Zone. I was not authorized to be here, and the sign at the entry way read, "**Authorized Military Personnel Only.**"

Promptly, the soldier took me down to the Provost Marshal's office. He reported to the clerk on duty what had happened, and that I was posing as an American. "This kid is not an American, he's a Kraut!" he said. I had no idea what was to happen next. Through my mind flashed the hangman's tree, **and I was scared. After waiting a few moments, the clerk advised the soldier that he had relayed his story about me to** the Provost Marshal, and that he would see me soon. Then the clerk excused the soldier. After several minutes, which seemed like hours, the clerk directed me to go into the Provost Marshal's office.

On the desk was the Provost Marshal's nameplate, Major Baumgartner. I was struck by this name because it was a German name. Behind the desk sat a rather large man, with several ribbons on his chest, armed with a sidearm, a .45 caliber pistol. I was impressed. I kept reflecting on his desk nameplate. It not only had his name but also had the crossed pistols insignia of the U.S. Military Police. Major Baumgartner began questioning me. The Major's questions followed by my responses are shown in the following dialogue:

Question: What is your name?
Answer: Arthur D. Jacobs.

Question: Where do you live?
Answer: 111 Langenwischstrasse, Stickgras by Delmenhorst.

Question: What brought you to this facility?
Answer: I was looking for work.

Question: What sort of work were you looking for?
Answer: Any work that was available.

Question: How old are you?
Answer: I turned 14 last month.

Question: Where are your parents?
Answer: They live at the same address I do.

Question: Do you have any brothers or sisters?
Answer: Yes, I have one brother.

Question: What is his name?
Answer: Lambert W. Jacobs. We call him Sonney.

Question: How old is he?

Answer: He is two years older than I am.

These questions were directed in rapid-fire succession. After I responded to each, the Major would jot down some notes. Sometimes he would pause and then begin another round of questioning.

Question: Where were you born?
Answer: Wyckoff Heights Hospital, Brooklyn, New York

Question: Where was your brother born?
Answer: In the same hospital as I was.

Question: What are you doing in Germany?
Answer: After the war my parents volunteered to repatriate to Germany, and my brother and I had to go with them.

Question: Where were you before you came to Germany?
Answer: Ellis Island, New York Harbor, New York.

Question: What were you doing there?
Answer: We were interned there while we waited for a shipping date.

Question: When did you leave the United States?
Answer: We left on January 17, 1946 aboard the S.S. Aiken Victory.

Question: When did you arrive in Germany and where?
Answer: I arrived at the Port of Bremerhaven on January 26, 1946.

Question: Where did you go from there?
Answer: American soldiers loaded us into trucks and took us to Bremen.

Question: How long did you stay here (Bremen)?
Answer: I don't think we remained here long. We went through some sort of processing.

Question: Where did you go from Bremen?
Answer: American GIs loaded us into boxcars and took us to Ludwigsburg.

Question: In boxcars?
Answer: Yes, sir, in boxcars.

Question: When you arrived in Ludwigsburg, what did you do?
Answer: We remained under the control of the United States Army, by this I mean that we continued to be internees, prisoners so to speak. There we were unloaded. My mother went in one direction (I did not know where they took her). My father, brother, and I were loaded in a 2.5-ton truck and taken to a place called Hohenasperg.

Question: What did you do there?
Answer: I was a prisoner!

Question: What do you mean you were a prisoner?
Answer: A prisoner. I was placed in a cell. Anytime I was out of my cell I was under the watchful eye of an armed military guard. Yes, I was a prisoner, that is what I was, a prisoner.

```
Question:   Why were you put into prison?
Answer:     I don't know.  I've been asking myself
            this same question.  I asked it when I was
            in my cell, when I was released, and I'm
            still asking.
```

Major Baumgartner began asking the questions with less rapidity. As we proceeded, he took more and more notes, at least this was the impression I had. I thought he was rather surprised at how I replied to his questions without hesitation. My hands began to sweat, and I was very nervous. I was not concerned with the questions, for I knew the truth. My concern was what was in store for me when the Major was through with his questioning.

```
Question:   How long were you held prisoner in
            Hohenasperg?
Answer:     I don't know.  I just know each day was a
            day of torment.  (I was in hopes that if I
            told him how I suffered in Hohenasperg
            the Major would be lenient).

Question:   Why were you held there?
Answer:     I have no idea.  You'll have to ask the
            Army officials for an answer to that
            question.

Question:   When you were released from
            Hohenasperg what did you do?
Answer:     I just hung around Ludwigsburg and
            Stuttgart waiting for my mother and father
            to be released.

Question:   When was your father released?
Answer:     In the middle of March.
```

Question: After your father was released where did you go?

Answer: To where I live now in Stickgras.

Question: What have you been doing up until now?

Answer: I went to the German school for awhile. I quit because I did not like my teacher, the school, or the subjects. Then I had to get an Arbeitskarte. After I received my work card I found a job with the U.S. Army Graves Registration in Oldenburg.

Question: With the Graves Registration? What did you do for them?

Answer: Odds and ends. I interpreted, and I drove and put gas in vehicles.

Question: Do you have a driver's license?

Answer: No, sir.

Question: Why did you drive Army vehicles without a driver's license?

Answer: I don't know. I guess the soldiers trusted me to drive carefully and safely. I never had an accident.

Question: When you worked for the Graves Registration where did you live?

Answer: During the week I lived in a barrack at Oldenburg. On weekends, I generally lived at home.

Question: Before you were interned where did you live?

Answer: 411 Himrod Street, Brooklyn, New York.

Question: What school did you attend?

Answer:	P.S. 81 and before that I attended P.S. 106. Mr. Brill was my seventh grade teacher and Mrs. Lewis was my fifth grade teacher. I think Mr. Brill…

At this point the Major interrupted me. He said, "I didn't ask you who your teachers were I just wanted to know the names of your last school before internment. Just answer the questions." I was going to tell him that I thought Mr. Brill had served in the United States Army Air Corps, but I never had the opportunity to tell him about Mr. Brill.

Question:	Now tell me again, why were you in this barrack?
Answer:	Sir, I was looking for work.

Question:	Do you hang out in and around military facilities often?
Answer:	I don't hang around. I'm always there for a purpose, mainly to find a friend who will help me get back to America, and secondly to get work. As you know all males older than twelve must work if they want rations. If I don't work I cannot get my weekly supply of bread and milk.

Question:	What type of work can you do?
Answer:	I can do many odds and ends. As I told you I can drive. I can service vehicles, refuel, check the oil, and do a certain amount of greasing. I can do some interpretation. I have lots of work experience.

Question:	What do you mean you have lots of work experience?

Answer: When I lived in Brooklyn I did odd jobs
            for the corner grocer, the butcher, and for
            the coal, kerosene, and ice man. I also
            delivered the Brooklyn Eagle newspaper.
            So I have had responsibility collecting
            money on my route and paying my bills. I
            have also sold pretzels on the street
            corners of Brooklyn. On my own I
            bought my supply of pretzels. I know
            what it takes to make a profit. I also
            worked for the "vegetable" man. He
            would come by on Saturdays with his
            horse and wagon. His wagon would be
            loaded with fresh vegetables—potatoes,
            beans, onions, peas, cantaloupe and
            watermelons in season, carrots, beets,
            radishes, scallions, and fresh fruits. I
            would meet him at a certain corner then
            ride with him all day. Many of his
            customers would give him their orders
            from upper story flats, and I would then
            deliver the order to the customer's
            apartment, generally to the third floor. I
            would collect the appropriate amount, and
            make change as necessary. My wages
            would be tips and at the end of the day,
            the "vegetable" man would give me a
            quarter to boot. And as you know, over
            here I did some work for the Graves
            Registration.

While the Major was questioning me and as I was
responding, pleasant memories came to mind. I forgot about
the harsh winter, which had just passed and thought about
my friends and classmates in Brooklyn. My focus at this
time of the questioning was not in Germany, or even in
Bremen, but it was back in my old neighborhood of

Brooklyn. To the place where my hopes and dreams had been shattered by officials of the United States Government. But I quickly came back to reality, and I had to be careful not to daydream. The Major expected prompt replies.

I kept wondering how much longer the questioning would go on. The longer it lasted the more nervous I became. I was not offered any water or anything to drink or eat during this entire ordeal.

Question: Do you have proof that you are an American citizen?

Answer: No. But last December I applied for a passport at the American Consulate here in Bremen.

Question: Did the consulate issue you a passport?

Answer: No.

Question: Do you know why they haven't issued you a passport?

Answer: I have no idea. Sir, you need to understand that my government, the United States Government, sent me over here without papers. My citizenship has been denied! I am a boy without a country! My only papers are my "Meldekarte"[16] from the Arbeitsamt[17].

---

[16] A "Meldekarte" was proof that you were employed or in school. In effect it was a registration card upon which the central labor office would certify that you were employed and your employer would sign the card to show proof that you were gainfully employed. A very bureaucratic process.

[17] Translated: Labor Office

The Major immediately told me to show him my "Meldekarte." I knew I should not have mentioned this document. Now the Major will know that I live in the British Occupation Zone and that I am in Bremen without proper authorization. The Major examined my card, jotted down some notes, and then without a word he returned my card to me. I thought that if I hadn't told the Major about my "Meldekarte" that most of the questioning would have been over. The Major rotated his chair with his back to me so that he was facing the window. I did not say a word, I just sat there. After some minutes the Major turned to me and started to lecture me.

His lecture started with, "I don't want to ever see you in my office again. You are not to enter any military barrack in this enclave unless you have an official authorization to do so. If you do, I will have you arrested!"

> Question: Do you understand?
> Answer: Yes, sir!

Furthermore, the Major said, "From now on you, like all other citizens of Germany, you must abide by the rules."

> Question: Do you understand?
> Answer: Yes, sir, but I'm not a German. I am an
>   American!

The Major replied in a loud voice, "It makes no difference what you think your citizenship is. As far as we, the Military Government are concerned, you are a German citizen. And you do not have any special privileges."

> Question: Do you understand?
> Answer: Yes, sir!

I was dismissed with the Major's final words of advice, "From now on abide by the rules." I was relieved, and I thanked the Major for allowing me to leave.

I walked out of the building thinking that this episode was over. I was appreciative that I was not imprisoned, placed in a stockade or sent back to Hohenasperg. I could not have again borne the sight of the hangman's tree. I proceeded on foot toward the catwalk footbridge. As I was walking I noticed a car that appeared several times at different places during my walk. I developed a photographic image of the automobile and the driver. When I arrived at the footbridge, I waited until several people arrived and we crossed the bridge together. The automobile I spotted earlier remained in my view. As usual, I passed the sentry without a hitch. When I reached the other side, I breathed a sigh of relief.

After I arrived home I hung out in front of my Opa's house. It was nearing the supper hour, but it was still daylight. As I stood by our front gate, I noticed the vehicle and driver, that had been following me, coming up our street. As the vehicle neared me, I acted as if I did not even notice it. A very short while later the vehicle came back in the other direction. Again, I ignored the vehicle's approach. By this time, I was convinced that the driver of the vehicle had tailed me. Of course, I thought, it was Major Baumgartner who had me followed. I was confused. Why would the Provost Marshal have a kid like me followed? Did he consider me dangerous? Why this? Was he trying to catch me doing something wrong? I had been honest with the Major. I told him who I was, where I lived, where I came from, and so forth. However, after I went into the house, I was glad to put the events of the day behind me. Maybe my imagination was getting the best of me.

A day or two later, I was sitting on the railing in front of our house, when the man who had followed me home a few days before, appeared. I don't think he knew that I was aware that he had followed me. He pulled his car off the road, and asked me in German for directions to Delmenhorst:

Question: How do I get to Delmenhorst?[18]
Answer: Turn right here.

Question: Do you live in this vicinity?
Answer: "Yes, I live in this house," as I pointed to my Opa's house.

Question: How come you have a foreign accent?
Answer: I was born in America. I am an American. I have only been in Germany for a short while.

Question: What does your father do for work?
Answer: My father works in the peat fields.

Question: Do you go to school?
Answer: No, sir.

Question: How do you get your rations?
Answer: I was working for the United States Army Graves Registration.

At this point I became anxious because I had not reported to the "Arbeitsamt" that I was unemployed and I had been certifying that I was working while I was looking for work. I was fearful that the agent would uncover my wrongdoing and report it back to the Major. I was now convinced that Major Baumgartner had me followed.

---

[18] There were two direction signs directly in his view on Sykestrasse. One sign pointed to the east and the other pointed to the west. Both signs, however, had been shot up during the war and remained illegible.

Question: Do you go to Bremen?
Answer: Often.

Question: What type of pass do you have to go into Bremen?
Answer: None.

At this point I was growing tired of the questions. I had to think of something to get him "off my back."

Question: Are you an American citizen?
Answer: Yes, sir!

Question: Do you have proof of your citizenship?
Answer: No, sir!

Question: Why don't you have proof?

This question was an opening for me to start playing my game with the agent, and I answered as follows:

Answer: Sir, I'm not supposed to tell you this, but this is the only way I can explain it. Really, I shouldn't be telling you this, as I was not to know what I am about to tell you. Several weeks ago I overheard a private conversation that my father was having with my mother. In this conversation my father told my mother that he was a Special Secret Agent for the United States. This is the only part of the conversation I heard.

Question: You say your father is a secret agent of the American government? Are you sure?

Answer: Yes, sir. I'm certain. I hope that you will not tell anyone else about this. I will be in trouble if you do. I really shouldn't have told you about this, but I could no longer keep it a secret.

I had the impression as the agent prepared to leave that he was delighted that he had uncovered that my father was a secret agent for the United States Government. He was, in my opinion, anxious to report his latest findings to Major Baumgartner.

The weather continued to improve, and daily it became a bit warmer. I had become somewhat complacent, and I did not want to find work. One reason for my reluctance was that I thought I would be restricted to work for either the British or in the local economy. My relationship with Germans was not the best; as a matter of fact, it was antagonistic. The feelings were mutual. They had no use for me, as I was the victor, and I had no use for them. They were the enemy. Most of the Germans in positions of authority, whom I had to deal with were rude and obnoxious. They would be delighted when they found fault with my required weekly registration and/or my actions. Each time I went to the Labor Office it was like being thrashed mentally. It got to the point that I did not want to report to the Labor Office as required. Ultimately, I even feared going to the office, so I stayed home.

I helped my Opa in the garden. Everything we did we used hand tools, spades, hoes and rakes. We made asparagus mounds, and fertilized the strawberry plants. We planted potatoes and a host of other vegetables. As far as I was concerned my Opa was a pro at gardening. He knew what had to be done, when it had to be done, and he worked side by side with me. He and I joked a lot. I remember the previous summer when it was time to pick the strawberries.

Opa said to me, "Now when we pick the strawberries, you must whistle." "Opa," I asked, "why must I whistle when I pick the berries?" He replied, "Because when you stop whistling, I will know you have eaten a strawberry." If it had not been for my Opa during my second spring in Germany I don't think I would have survived.

At the dinner table he was always good for a laugh. He was the "lighter side of my life." You could tell Opa had been through hard times before, and he knew these hard days would also pass. One of my most memorable lighter and lasting moments came at dinnertime. The caloric values of most of our foods were nil. Opa, my parents and my brother and I had just sat down at the table. We waited for Oma to bring in the turnip soup. Just as Oma appeared with the tureen of soup, a fly appeared in the room. Oma said to Opa, "There's a fly, get it before it flies into the soup." Opa caught the fly, and my brother said, "Opa, throw it into the soup. Calories, you know." Opa burst out laughing. I had never seen him laugh so much. For the first time I sensed a real smile on the face of my Oma, and she began to laugh at my brother's suggestion. From that day forward anytime we saw a fly while we were eating, the word was "kalorein."[19] Those were the days.

---

[19] Translated: calories

Chapter Sixteen

Angels from Kansas

I continued helping my Opa in the garden for the remainder of the spring. In early June or late May of 1947, I was standing outside the front gate of my Opa's house when I saw a U.S. Army jeep heading in my direction. The first thing I noticed about the jeep was that the bumper contained the initials **CIC**. I knew that those initials were the abbreviation for the Army's Counter Intelligence Corps. The driver was an army sergeant. He first passed by our house, but in a few minutes he came back and stopped in front of the house. I just knew I was in serious trouble. Many events crossed my mind. One was the story that my father was a U.S. Secret Agent that I told to the agent that Major Baumgartner had follow me. My unlawful entries into Bremen came to mind. The fact that I had not worked as I should have for several weeks. Why is this sergeant stopping here?

The sergeant got out of the jeep and approached me. I felt like running, but there was no place to run. I had backed myself into a corner. Visions of Hohenasperg and the hangman's tree flashed before me. I heard someone yell "you little Nazi." The sound of the cell door closing rung in my ears. All my living nightmares flashed before me in an instant. I was scared.

The soldier asked, "Are you Arthur D. Jacobs?" In a nervous voice I told him that I was. He introduced himself as Sergeant Davies of the CIC Motor Pool. Then he said, "We have heard that you are looking for a job." I told him I was. "We have work for you in the CIC Motor Pool in Bremen. You will have to come with me to fill out the paperwork and get your passes." I wondered. Is this a way for them to capture me? Or is this for real? But, I thought I had nothing to lose, so I went along with him.

On the way into Bremen, Sergeant Davies asked me many questions. Question like I had heard so often. Why are you in Germany? How did you get here? Where were you born? Where were you before you came to Germany? How long have you been in Germany?

I told the sergeant how my father was interned and how our home was ransacked several times by the FBI. I even told him that I begged officials to release my father. "Sergeant Davies," I said, "someone made a mistake when they arrested my father." I told him that my father brought up my brother and me to be patriots of the United States.

When we arrived at the Motor Pool, I filled out the papers. Sergeant Davies checked my work card and signed it and issued me a pass that allowed me to travel to and from Bremen on a daily basis. No longer would I have to have trepidation when crossing the river. I was now legal! Then he showed me around the motor pool. The motor pool was nothing more than four of five single car garages that were converted into a mechanic's garage. Two or three soldiers, along with several German civilians who were mechanics, were employed in the shop. Minor maintenance, refueling, and oil checks were the primary responsibilities of the garage. The CIC office was directly across the street. After I was through with my orientation, Sergeant Davies took me home.

I remained unsure of this situation. After I arrived at my home I had several lingering questions. Was I hired because the CIC needed me or was I given this job so that Major Baumgartner could keep tabs on me? Sergeant Davies gave me no indication as to why I was hired, and I did not ask. I was content to be employed. Most important I again had the opportunity to be among Americans. I remained skeptical, but I performed my job well.

Most of my duties involved checking the oil and water in the jeeps and staff cars, including a pre-World War II BMW roadster. Typically I would, as necessary, add oil and water, clean the windshields, and wash the vehicle. When the agents came to the office and their vehicle needed service, they would drop off their keys and their trip tickets in the motor pool indicating the necessary service. We would hang the keys up on the service board in the order that they arrived and service the vehicles accordingly.

When the CIC agents dropped off their vehicles I attempted to greet all of those in uniform. My aim was to let them know that I was an American. Most of them would do a double-take when they heard my English spoken without a German accent. A few would ask, "How come you speak such good English?" My reply always included, "I am an American." Sometimes an agent would question me a bit further and then go on about his business. Other times there would be a "hmmm" and that was it.

After I had been there several weeks, a lady drove up to the garage. This was the first time I had met the wife of an agent. I started to greet her, but before I could get the words out of my mouth, she asked in German, with the expression and tone of a concerned person, "What are your doing here? Why aren't you in school?" I replied, "You can speak English to me, I am an American." "You are what?" she asked. Here we go again, I thought. I am about to get grilled. I replied, "Ma'am I am an American." I started to service her vehicle, but this was not to be. The lady held out her hand and said, "Hi, I am Mary Simmons and I am pleased to meet you." With my dirty hands, I shook her hand and gave her my name. I gave her a condensed version of my story, and much to my surprise, I could tell by her facial expressions that she believed me. I had met someone who had trust in me. Then Mary continued the questioning. She wanted to know where my parents and I lived. I told her that we lived across the river in the British Zone.

The subject got back to school. Mary told me that she was a former Kansas schoolteacher, and she said, "You should be in school." I told her, "I prefer to work. I tried school and could not get along with my teacher." "How old are you?" she asked, and I told her I was fourteen. "Do you have any brothers or sisters?" she asked. I replied, "I have a brother who is about two years older than I am." Then she asked, "Where does he live?" I said, "With my parents, and he has been working with U.S. Army Mortuary Service at Cochem on the Mosel River, but I think that work has ended and he is looking for work. My brother always has liked school, and he would probably like to be tutored." After Mary was finished with her questions, I told her that my brother and I wanted to go back to the United States. I said, "My number one goal is to go back to the good old U.S. of A." She seemed to understand. Then she told me that she would discuss her "finding" with her husband Edwin, and she took down my address and left.

The very next weekend, Mary and her husband, Agent Edwin Simmons, drove up to our house. We had no idea they were coming. I recognized Mary right away, but at this time I did not know her husband. I called for my parents and brother to come downstairs, because we had company.

After my parents had come outside, Mary took on the responsibility of introductions. She started by introducing herself and her husband to my parents and my brother. Then she turned to me and said, "Archie (my nickname), this is my husband, Edwin." I remembered she told me that she would have a discussion with her husband about me. After the introductions were over, my mother invited the Simmons into our home. The Simmons obliged and went upstairs and I followed. My mother invited them to have a seat and asked if they would like to have a cup of coffee. Both responded, "Yes." Mom started the coffee, set the table and asked them to make themselves at home. While the coffee was brewing all of us sat around the dining table and talked.

Mary told us that she was a schoolteacher and could tutor both of us. She asked my brother if he would like to be tutored, and he said, "I like the idea." I told her that I preferred to work because I needed to meet as many people as I could to find a way back to America. Questions from my mother to Mary and vice versa took over the conversation for quite some time. Both acted as if they had known each other for years. Likewise there was considerable conversation between Agent Simmons and my father. All of us enjoyed the warmth and heartfelt concern that Mary expressed to my mother. Mary told my mother how important it was for her two sons to complete their formal education. My mother explained how much I personally disliked going to the local German school in our neighborhood. Mary again reiterated that she was a schoolteacher and could satisfactorily teach my brother and me the fundamentals that we are missing at this stage of our development.

When the coffee was ready, my mother excused herself and got up from the table. She set the table with coffee cups, saucers, spoons, sugar, and milk. As my mother was setting the table, Mary said to both of my parents, "I have friends in southwest Kansas who own a wheat ranch, and these people have a sincere interest in the welfare of children. As a result they have recently adopted five children. They have plenty of room on their 10,000-acre ranch where children can lead a wholesome life. I know them quite well, and with your permission I will ask them if they would like to take in both of your sons."

My mother was taken off guard, and immediately got tears in her eyes. Then Mom said, "I do not want my boys to leave home, they are so young. They will be so far away from here. What will the boys do if they get homesick or if they don't like it there? You know, they have always lived in a big city, until we moved here. Neither one of my boys likes living in the country. They are always going off into the cities. What do you boys think?" I told my parents and Mary and Ed that I wanted to go back to the States. I said, "Mom and Pop, I want to go back in the worst way." I am sure my brother agreed, but he did not say much. I did most of the talking. Even though I wanted to get excited about this possibility of my dream coming true, I was denied so long that I was still suspicious. In the back of my mind I was wondering if this was really happening, is it true, or are the Simmons agents of Major Baumgartner? The pros and cons of my brother and me returning to the States were the topics of discussion for more than two hours. My father, for the most part, just listened to the discussion. Shortly before the discussion ended, my father turned to my mother and said, "Mom, let the boys go back to their country. If they don't go today, they will go tomorrow." My mother tried to smile, but tears rolled down her cheeks. She lifted her handkerchief to her cheeks, wiped away the tears, turned her face to my father, and said, "But Pop, they are so young and will be so far away, and to whom will they turn for help?" Tears continued to roll down her cheeks, and then I also noticed tears in Mary's eyes. Pop replied, "Let them go, Mom."

Mom then turned her eyes toward me, "Archie," she said, "do you really want to go? Sonney, do you really want to go?" Both of us nodded our heads, and said, "Yes!" Mom turned her head towards Pop once again, and said, "It looks like we are going to lose our boys." Pop said, "Mom, think about it this way. The boys will be so much better off in America. They have nothing here. The people here are not nice to the boys, and Archie is always getting into trouble. The boys have lost nothing over here. We let them go, okay?" Another smile came across Mom's face, and with her eyes filled with tears, she replied, "Okay Pop, the boys can go."

At that point Ed immediately stepped into the conversation, and said with authority and without hesitation, "Mr. and Mrs. Jacobs you made the right decision for your boys. There is nothing here for them. They need to continue their education, and perhaps you will be able to join them soon." Mary nodded her head in the affirmative and said, "Both of you have had to make a hard choice, but I think it is the correct one. I think we will go home now and let you and your family continue this discussion. I will write my friends in Kansas about your situation." Ed and Mary left.

My parents, my brother and I continued to sit around the dining table and discuss the matter. I was getting excited and my exhilaration over the events of the afternoon must have been evident to my father. He said, "Don't get your hopes up too high, because nothing is for sure yet. Much has to be done." I said, "Pop, this is what I have been yearning for ever since we arrived in Germany. I just don't like it here."

I continued to work at the CIC motor pool as I awaited word from Kansas. Each day that I would see either Ed Simmons or his wife Mary, I would ask, "Have you heard anything?" Sometime during the month of September, Mary drove up to the motor pool, stopped, got out of her vehicle, and said, "Archie, I have good news. Art and Mildred Dreyer, my friends in Kansas, have agreed to help you and your brother get back to the United States." Mary went on to tell me that they not only agreed to help us get back, but that they would also provide for us when we get there. In other words we would become part of their family. I was speechless, my dream has almost come true. "What next?" I asked, with great excitement.

Mary said the first thing we must do is to get the Dreyer's letter and you and your brother to the consulate to work on obtaining your passport. My brother was already at the Simmons residence getting tutored, and I excused myself from work so I could go with Mary. I told Sergeant Davies that I was going back to the States. He asked, "What, you are going back to the States?" "Yes!" I said. He said, "That's great news Archie. Congratulations, I'm happy for you." Mary and I drove off to her home, picked up my brother and went directly to the American Consulate. A German national, who asked, "May I help you?" greeted us. Mary showed her the letter from the Dreyers and told her that these boys, pointing at us, are Americans and that they had applied for a passport last December.

As usual the German clerk took on an aura of bureaucracy. First, she read the entire letter from the Dreyers. Then, in broken English she said, "This will not do, we have particular forms that must be completed." Mary in her most charming and tactful way, said, "Oh, that's fine, just give us the forms and I will have my husband, who is with the Army Counter Intelligence Corps, have them completed." The clerk stuttered and cleared her throat a time or two and then responded, "I will have to check with my chief." To which Mary replied, "That will be fine, go right ahead, we have plenty of time." Then Mary again said, "You know these two boys are American citizens. Please inform your chief of this when you talk to him."

The clerk had been away for only a moment or two, when she returned with her supervisor. He too was a German national, and a bit arrogant in his manner, when he said, "How can I help you?" Mary said, "Good morning I am

Mary the dependent wife of Agent Ed Simmons of the Army Counter Intelligence Corps Detachment here in Bremen. My husband and I have obtained a sponsorship and fare for these two boys to return to the United States. I am here to complete the necessary processing. Is there a problem?" Like the clerk, the supervisor was not sure of himself. "We will have to look into this matter," he stated. At this point I was reminded of my experiences with the obnoxious clerk in the Delmenhorst Labor Office. I concluded that the Germans who worked in high places did two things; abused their power and basically disliked Americans.

Mary responded, "What do you have to look into? These American boys want to return home to their country. They are Americans. You already know this because they applied for their passport almost a year ago." In a stern voice Mary asked, "Why haven't they been issued a passport?" Then Mary told the supervisor, "You have all the paperwork, now please get their files. On second thought, let us speak to the U.S. Foreign Service Officer."

The supervisor left and came back with an American Foreign Service Officer of the U.S. State Department. The officer asked how he could help us. Mary explained, "It is quite simple." The Foreign Service Officer interrupted Mary, and said, "Let's go to my office." We followed him to his office. When we got to the office, the officer immediately asked the supervisor to pull the records on the Jacobs' passport application. After we sat down, Mary explained to him why she was there. She also presented the letter to him that she had received from the Dreyers in Kansas. He then read the letter. The supervisor returned with our passport application, which he handed to the consulate officer. He examined the applications, then looked up and said, "I see no problem. The consulate will issue the passport when proof is shown that they have tickets and a $600.00 surety fee so that when they return to the United States, they will have sufficient funds to get to where they are going." Mary said, "That will be no problem." We thanked the officer for his help and left. As we were leaving, the two German nationals we had made contact with earlier avoided eye contact with us as we left the building, but they watched our every move.

In a few weeks, Mary had obtained the necessary funds in travelers' checks. On October 29, 1947 we were to set sail for the United States aboard the American Ship Lines passenger ship, the Marine Flasher. This was a very exciting time for me.

My brother and I proceeded to the American Consulate to pick up our passports. When we walked in the door there was the same German clerk, who had done a lousy job the first time. She began with a bunch of questions, do you have this document and that document? Each document she asked for we placed upon the counter. Then she said, "I must check these documents thoroughly. You can leave them here." I said, "No! We will not leave the documents here. These documents are our ticket to America." I must have been a bit loud, because the Consul General came to the counter. He asked, "Is there a problem here?" I said, "Not as far as I'm concerned. The clerk said we had to leave our documents while she checked them out. I told her that we weren't going to let these documents out of our hands."

The Consul General picked up the documents, examined them, and then said, "Just a moment." He came back with his pen in hand and completed the passport. Then he added the seal of the Consulate of Bremen, Germany, and affixed the appropriate stamp. When he was done, he had my brother sign the passport. The Consul General made it a point to congratulate both my brother and me, and said, "Bon Voyage!"

It seemed that all the loose ends were tied together, but time did not go by fast enough for me. However, the days were passing by too fast for my mother. During our last few days my mother reminisced a good part of the time.

She talked about the time when my brother first started to school and I followed him. My mother had not known I had slipped off with him. When I arrived at the school, a teacher, who knew that I was a bit young and shouldn't be there, intercepted me. The teacher pinned a note on my shirt and told me to go home and give the note to my mother.

Then Mom recalled the time I had four of my fingers stuck in a toy, each one in a different hole. I was sick at home in bed when this happened. I had been trying to get my fingers out of the contraption, but they began to swell. When my mother came into the room, she quickly noticed that my fingers were swollen, discolored, purple and blue. Outside of my bedroom window there was a fire alarm, and Mom yelled out the window to a person who happened to be standing there to pull the alarm. The alarm was pulled, and because our apartment was in a high-rise, the hook and ladder truck responded to the alarm. In came a fireman, who looked at my hand and immediately got tin snips out and cut the toy from around my fingers. My fingers were saved!

Mom even brought up the incident when I had asked her to sew on the letters for my team's baseball shirts. Then she recounted the time I mixed cement on my aunt's front stoop. For the next ten days we all reminisced. We laughed a lot during those ten days, but Mom would laugh, then cry. Sometimes at night I could hear her crying. Each morning I would try to get her to think about better and happier times. My father would also try to console her. He would tell her to just think how much better off the boys will be over there— in the States.

A couple of days before we left, all of us agreed that it would be best for our parents to stay home and not join us at the pier on the day we left. We did this because we thought it would be less painful for Mom, and because they would not be allowed to enter the American Shipping Lines processing building.

Chapter Seventeen

Home at Last!

On the day we left, Mom made sure we looked sharp, and helped us check and double check to make certain that we had put all of the things we would need in our luggage. After a final hug and kiss, Mom became speechless, her cheeks wet with tears. Just moments before we left, Pop said, "Boys! Archie and Sonney, have a safe trip!" Then he turned to Mom, and said, "Don't worry, it won't be long and we will see our boys again." Mom tried to smile. Then she put my dog, Suzie, on the ground, reached into her little pocketbook, pulled out her white handkerchief and began to wave it as she had on the Ellis Island Ferry. I kept my eye on the waving handkerchief until it was out of sight. Hope, whispering hope!

Off to Bremen we went. I can recall nothing about our ride into Bremen and over to the port. I do remember that when we got there we had to enter a large building. The building was closely guarded and only passengers, persons with tickets and a passport, were allowed to enter. We entered the building, sat down with our luggage and waited for our ship's name to be called. We arrived a bit early so we had to wait for about an hour. Finally, they called for passengers to board the Marine Flasher. We picked up our luggage and proceeded to the line. Once we were in line, health personnel checked our inoculation records. We cleared that hurdle. The next station examined our tickets and issued us baggage claim tickets for our baggage. At the last station our passport (I was on the same passport as my brother) was examined. When we passed this station I said, "Hurray" and ran up the gangplank. Immediately someone shouted, "Please no running." I stopped running and walked the rest of the way at a fast pace. Once on board we were shown our quarters and handed a schedule of events. I thought, "At last, it's happening! My dream, it's coming true."

I remember very little about the voyage. Unlike my voyage aboard the S.S. Aiken Victory, this trip was rather dull and boring. But I didn't care, I was finally going home. I remember telling other children who were on board that I was going home. "What do you mean going home?" some asked. Most of the other children were German and other European children who were coming to America for the first time. I said, "America is my home." As usual I had difficulty explaining my situation to others. Finally, I simply gave up, ignored the rest of the passengers and just counted the days.

It was nighttime when we entered New York Harbor. I remember how glad I was to see the Statue of Liberty once again. I could also see the New York skyline and even glimpses of Ellis Island. We spent the night anchored in the harbor.

The next morning we docked at one of the New York piers, and a few moments later we were disembarking. I never looked back. Once I was off the gangplank I knew I was free at last. "Free," I said. No more passes, no more guards, no more reporting to the Labor Office. Now I can go into any store and buy what I want, when I want.

We hailed a taxi and said, "Grand Central Station, please." At Grand Central Station we boarded our assigned train and headed west. The trip as I remember was not exciting until we changed trains at Kansas City. At Kansas City we changed to a "milk run" train, as it was called. We stopped at places that didn't even have a train station. At one of the small town stops, the conductor of the train came by and told my brother and me, who were the only passengers on the train, that the train would be there long enough to get lunch at the local café. So we got off and walked with the train's crew over to the café. Here we had our first experience with Kansas hospitality. Not only were the members of the crew friendly, but the operators of the café, who had never seen us before, acted as if we were old friends. I was impressed.

Once we left this small town, it seemed that at each stop the train would halt before it even got to a full head of steam. At most of the stations, a member of the crew would unload a package or two and pick up other packages. Initially this was interesting, but after awhile, it too got old. After many, many stops, we arrived at the Garden City Station in Kansas—our destination.

When my brother and I stepped off the train, there was no one on the platform, nor was there anyone in the passenger waiting area, which consisted of two or three wooden high-backed benches—nothing like New York's Grand Central Station. We looked in front of the station for Mr. Dreyer, but he was not there. The only thing we could do was wait. I noticed that the street and parking area in front of the station was not paved, like the streets of Brooklyn.

A short while after we arrived at the station, a big man came into the passenger waiting area. He was dressed in a pair of blue and white striped denim coveralls. I thought he was a railroad engineer. He looked at us and we looked at him, and neither of us spoke. Then he asked, "Are you the German boys?" Oh no, I thought to myself, he thinks we are German! Didn't Mary tell Mr. Dreyer that we are Americans? I thought, I am going to have to go through this again, trying to explain to him that I am an American, not a German. I replied, "No! We are American boys who came back from Germany." Then Mr. Dreyer said, seeing a little fire in my eyes, "I'm sorry, I should have asked, are you the boys who came from the old country?" I later learned that

116

Mr. Dreyer's roots go back to Germany, and in his family they referred to Germany as the "old country." Then he held out his hand and said, "I am Art Dreyer, welcome to Kansas." Both my brother and I shook his hand and thanked him for agreeing to take us in. We gathered up our luggage and walked out front to Mr. Dreyer's car, a new blue-gray 1947 Frazer. I was awestruck by the looks of the car. I had never seen such a car before. He opened up the trunk, and we put our luggage in. Then Mr. Dreyer closed the trunk, and said, "Both of you can ride in the front seat." The interior of the car was plush, and the seats were really comfortable, particularly after the wooden seats on the train from Kansas City to Garden City. During the next couple of hours the open range, that was all around us, overwhelmed me.

While we rode, I thought about how Mr. Dreyer welcomed us to Kansas. How much different, I thought, his welcoming was from the greeting we received from my uncle who met us at the Hauptbahnhof in Bremen. I thought, this man is sincere and genuine. I am going to like him. He has a presence about him that gives me the impression he is in charge, and he is kind and friendly. I wondered why he went to all of the trouble to get my brother and me back to the United States?

When I wasn't distracted by the bleak surroundings on both sides of the highways, I'd say to myself, "I sure like this car!"

Chapter Eighteen

My New Home—My New Family

The first thing I noticed as we left Garden City and were on the highway was how far I could see, and how barren the land seemed to be. It was a cold, gray, overcast November day. There were no trees. Nothing but dirt, wheat stubble, and a few patches of green. Sometimes the fields in front of us looked like the patchwork of a quilt. Despite the slow rolling hills in the area, you could see for miles and miles. I remember saying to Mr. Dreyer, "This sure is flat country." "Sure is, he replied, "and it's going to get flatter." At the time I did not know how far it was to the ranch, but it was just over one hundred miles from Garden City.

While he was driving, Mr. Dreyer attempted to give us a sense of direction. He said that we would be driving so many miles south and this many miles west and so forth. I thought this was odd. I was accustomed to talking about lefts, rights, and blocks, and Mr. Dreyer talked in terms of east, west, north and south, and miles. He asked few questions. He did however, ask about our voyage across the ocean and our train ride to Kansas. He must have known about the "milk run" train we were on because one of the questions he asked was, "Did the train stop often enough for you once you left Kansas City?" "Sure did," I replied. He smiled. I learned through this exchange and others while we were in the car that Mr. Dreyer had an excellent sense of humor. After we had been driving for some time, the panoramic view became bleaker and bleaker. There were still no trees, but now not even power lines or telephone poles. I was quickly becoming homesick for Mom and Pop. I thought back to when my mother asked me whether I was sure about going. Doubts were beginning to set in. We had been driving for more than an hour and there had been nothing to see. It seemed with each passing minute we were getting farther away from civilization, as I knew it. When we were about ten miles from the ranch I asked Mr. Dreyer "How much farther do we have to go?" "Ten miles," he replied. Wow, I thought to myself, this ranch is a long, long way out in the country. The only things to be seen were fence posts and barbed wire, and flat land. There were periods during our trip I didn't even see a fence post—it was so barren. When we crossed a cattle guard for the first time, I wondered what those spaced railroad track looking things were doing in the road. As we passed over it, Mr. Dreyer noted that we just crossed a cattle guard. "Two more to go and we will be at the ranch," he said. Now things were absolutely looking forbidding to me. As we crossed the second cattle guard, Mr. Dreyer informed us that we had three miles to go. The next three miles were flat, flat, and flatter. This is when I learned there was no commercial power on the ranch, and that the Dreyer's generated their own electric power with a Kohler generator.

When we were about two miles from our destination, I sighted the ranch buildings on the horizon against the otherwise bleak flat land of Kansas. It was then called and ever will be in my memory "The Ranch." As we got closer I saw the huge round top barn—a Quonset shaped structure. When we got to the ranch, Mr. Dreyer turned to the right over the third cattle guard. Then he drove the Frazer into the round top barn. Home! And free at last! Best of all my dream of coming home to America had come true!

There to greet us were Mildred, Art Dreyer's wife, and their five adopted children—two girls and three boys. All were younger than my brother and I, except one of the boys and he was my age. We were welcomed with open arms, and it made me feel good. We were shown our room, which was upstairs in the round top bunkhouse. I noticed to the right

119

and at the foot of the stairs there were several sheepskin-lined coats. The bunkhouse was not fancy, but it was neat and clean. I saw an old-time windup Victrola record player as we went upstairs. After we put our luggage away, we were shown the outhouse (outside toilet) and then we were taken to the wash house. It included a sink and a shower. The wash house was located about fifty feet to the east of the round top and right next to the windmill and stock tank. The Kohler electric generator was also in the wash house, and the heat from the engine kept the wash house warm.

After we were shown around all of the other buildings, the horse barn, the cow barn, the chicken coop, and the pigsty, we washed up and went into the dining room.

Immediately we were welcomed into the family. We had dinner and visited for a bit, and then it was time to go to bed. I looked out from the barn before I went up to my bed in the bunkhouse. There was not a light to be seen, or a noise to be heard except for the Kohler generator. When it went off, there was complete silence. Suddenly, I panicked. I kept asking myself why I wanted to come here? I was homesick, and I missed my mother and father. For the first time since I left Germany I longed to be with my parents.

The next morning I was up bright and early. I found paper and pencil and wrote a letter to my parents. In the letter, I told them I was homesick. I mentioned to them that the ranch was far away from anything, and at night you cannot see any lights. You can only see the stars in the sky. I told my parents there are no trees out here and the ranch is huge—more than 10,000 acres. In my own way, I attempted to describe my new family and culture. Customs were different; there was less formality and more congeniality. Adults and children seem to be on a first-name basis. "The Dreyers," I said, "are very pleasant people." Then I wrote that Mrs. Dreyer said they would call me "Arch" instead of

"Art" because Mr. Dreyer is referred to as "Art." So now I had a new nickname, "Arch." I told my parents it is a bit difficult for me to call my elders by their first name, but that I am sure I will get accustomed to it. I wrote, "Mrs. Dreyer prefers to be called Mildred, and Mr. Dreyer goes by Art or Boss." "Boss" is a term of endearment and respect, rather than one of authority."

For several days, I remained homesick, and I wrote my parents each day. Writing seemed to help me ease the pain of the homesickness. For two or three days I kept thinking over and over, did I make the correct decision when I left my parents? Should I have stayed with them in Germany until I was older?

Then one morning two or three days later and without notice, my homesickness was over. Simply gone. Vanished. I had settled in and found a place I could call home. My new family had accepted me. I was free! Here I had no fears as I had for the past twenty-one months in Germany. There were no border or zone guards here, and no one checked papers. That morning I knew that my decision to leave Germany was the right one. I continued to write to my parents, but sometimes the Boss and Mildred would have to remind me that I needed to answer my mother's letter—my mother did most of the writing. It would be a long eleven years before I saw my parents again.

After a week or two, we left the ranch to winter in the Dreyer's home in Kissimmee, Florida, where I enrolled in the eighth grade. We lived on a lake about ten miles from the school, and we commuted. Either the Boss or Mildred would shuttle us to school and pick us up after school. There was little opportunity for us to participate in after hours school activities. In the middle of March 1948, the Boss and I went back to the ranch. The rest of the family would return later. The Boss took me because I actually had a yearning to go with him and he was pleased. A few months earlier it would not have been my desire to go back there.

As soon as we arrived back at the ranch I enrolled in the eighth grade in the Richfield Kansas School. School was fourteen miles from the ranch, and in order to get to school, I obtained a driving permit that allowed me to drive to and from school in a Willys Jeep, a vehicle I had driven often in Germany. On the 12th of May, I graduated from the Richfield School. That summer I worked on the ranch as I did in the spring, chiseling and plowing the fields. The Boss made it clear that he had a great deal of confidence in my skills. During the summer he purchased a John Deere self-propelled combine in a community some ten miles from the ranch. He asked that I drive it home. I remember asking, "Who me?" He replied, "Yes, you." He noticed I was a bit hesitant and timid, and in his commanding voice he said, "Come on, you can do it." I was pleased he believed in me and it gave me confidence. I hopped on, started the engine, put it in gear, and headed for the ranch, and never looked back. It was one of my most gratifying moments since I had been on the ranch. Throughout harvest I was the combine driver—at age fifteen I was the youngest self-propelled combine driver in the county. (For almost 58 years now, 1999, I have called the ranch my home.) I loved Mildred and the Boss. They had invested in me for no earthly reason. Unselfishly they met my needs. I knew in my heart "They really loved me."

As summer was coming to an end, Mildred said it was time to think about high school. The nearest local high school was in Elkhart, Kansas, twenty-six miles from the ranch. Considering the distance and winter weather she did not think it would be wise for me to drive this distance each school day. She told me about The School of the Ozarks, a private school supported by donations and the Presbyterians, just outside of Branson, Missouri at Point Lookout. This appealed to me. I applied, was accepted and enrolled for the 1948 Fall Semester. I continued to go home to The Ranch for all holidays and summers. The Boss and Mildred were ever ready to "be there for me, in every way."

It was at the School of the Ozarks that I met my sweetheart, Viva Sims, who was scheduled to graduate in the Spring of 1951. I appealed for extra credits for my fluency in the German language, and carried extra credits during what should have been my Junior year, and graduated with my sweetheart and the Class of 1951.

In October, after trying to work fulltime and be a fulltime student at Kansas State University, I enlisted in the United States Air Force. In less than a year after my high school graduation, March 24, 1952, Viva and I were married while I was on leave from the United States Air Force and between duty stations.

I would continue to visit Mildred and the Boss throughout the remainder of their lives. I was one of "their sons." They were my "American parents," and were more than life to me. I was very fortunate to become a member of their family and to be loved by them. We will never know the untold story of what might have been had they not taken me in and cared for me body and soul. I am eternally in their debt and reserve the highest honor for both of them in my heart. My gratitude to them and to God has no measure! To God, to the Boss and Mildred, and to The Ranch for your love and for my life I stand at attention and Salute You!

Chapter Nineteen

Reunion

When I saw my mother and my father again for the first time in 1958, I had graduated from high school, enlisted in the Air Force, married my high school sweetheart, and was the father of two sons. Archie Keith was four and David Lee was six months old. I had just completed a two-year overseas tour of duty in Morocco, North Africa where my son David was born. Viva and I decided that rather than returning directly to the United States from Morocco we would return via an alternate port, Frankfurt, Germany.

It is very difficult for me to describe in words the look on the faces of both of my parents. Both were overjoyed, as were my wife and I. Tears of happiness rolled down the cheeks of my mother. After we had been there several days, I asked my mother a question that had been on my mind for eleven years. "Mom," I asked, "why did you go with Pop when he decided to return to Germany? "Archie," she replied, "when I married your father I vowed, 'until death do us part.' And your father told me that if I did not go back with him, that I would never see him again." I replied, "You should have told Pop, that you would not go, and that you and your sons would stay in America. Pop would not have returned to Germany." My mother said that he would have gone without his family. I disagreed.[20]

---

[20] Thirty years later I obtained a copy of my father's voluntary repatriation statement. In effect my father's statement said, "that if his wife refuses to accompany him to Germany, it would be his desire not to return to Germany."

Three years later in 1961, my mother visited us in the United States. Pop had a fear of flying at that time and he did not make the trip. During Mom's stay, I took her to my home, the ranch in Kansas. One of the first things Mom did when she arrived was to scoop up about four tablespoons of dirt, put them in a small cloth bag, and then tighten the bag's drawstring. I said, "Mom, why did you do that?" She replied, "I now have a part of the land where my sons lived when they were small boys." Mom then recalled some of the words from my homesick letters. One evening while we were sitting outside, Mom looked up toward the heavens and said, "Archie, look up, there are the stars you saw when you came here and which you wrote to me about when you were a small homesick boy in 1947." I replied, "Yes, Mom, those were my tough days, but I now know they were tougher for you and Pop."

Between 1970 and 1973, I was assigned duties at the Headquarters of the United States Air Forces in Europe (USAFE) at Wiesbaden, Germany. Viva, and our four children Archie (16), David (13), Dwayne (8) and Dianna (5) accompanied me during this three-year tour of duty. Wiesbaden is approximately ninety kilometers north of Kaiserslautern, Germany where my parents then resided. During the three years that we were stationed in Germany my family and I spent many precious moments with my parents and vice versa.

In 1974, my parents visited us in our home in Tempe, Arizona.[21] While they were here, I told them of one of my escapades as a boy in Germany. I said, the incident I am going to describe to you is the epitome of what I experienced

---

[21] After having had the privilege of serving my country for almost 22 years, I retired from the United States Air Force when I left Germany in 1973, and moved to Arizona.

during those trying, two years in Germany. "Endicott and Woods," I said, "allowed me to take their BMW motorcycle for a spin. I got on the motorcycle, started it, and drove it out of the driveway onto the cobblestone Bremer Strasse. I headed east toward the train station, but just as I passed the train station I caught a glimpse of a German Volkswagen police car in my rear view mirror. I immediately sped up. The faster I went the more frightened I became. The police were catching up, and I was so scared I made a quick U-turn and headed back to where I started. I thought I could elude the police, but they too made a U-turn and sped after me. I managed to keep some distance between us. When I got to the driveway I was driving a bit too fast, which caused me to skid into a wire fence. Fortunately, I was not injured and the motorcycle was not damaged. I continued through the driveway and parked the cycle out of site behind the house. Then I walked to the front of the house, and there were the police from which I thought I had so cleverly escaped. One of the German officers said to me in German, "Where is your driver's license?" I replied in broken German, "I no versteh Deutsch."[22] The officer continued to press me for information, and I continued to be evasive, to stall, and to pretend as if I didn't understand what he was saying. Finally, Endicott and Woods came to the front of the house and asked the police officers, "Was ist los?"[23] They, like me, acted as if they couldn't understand. The German police officers eventually became frustrated and angry, and departed in a huff.

This one event is symbolic of my situation as a boy in an uneasy, starving, and war-torn Germany. I became more wary the longer I remained in Germany, just as I became

---

[22] Translated: Don't understand German.
[23] Translated: What is the matter?

more frightened as I drove faster on that motorcycle to get away from the German officers.

I believe I was too German looking to be American, and too American minded to be German. During all of those months in Germany I was in a Catch-22 situation.

EPILOGUE

The old cliché, "Truth is Stranger Than Fiction," has certainly been confirmed by the World War II nightmare experience of thirteen-year-old Arthur D. Jacobs, an American boy trapped in war-ravaged Germany. His gripping story is told on the preceding pages. The fact that the author's abominable wartime treatment as a "young Nazi" at the hands of his own countrymen left no permanent psychological scars or bitter resentment is remarkable in itself. As his long-time friend, I can attest that, to his lasting credit, the opposite has been true.

As the foregoing story tells us, Arthur was a minor child of permanent resident alien[24] (German) parents and an American citizen whose father was interned during World War II. With the loss of family support, Arthur's mother had no choice but to join her husband in internment, taking with her two minor sons who had no other means of support. Thus we are taken with the Jacobs family on the sad journey which ended in devastated Germany, a hostile land which young Arthur had never seen and from which he tried desperately to find a way home to America. After a long, hard struggle and dogged perseverance he managed to do so.

Arthur finally saw his parents after many years of separation during the formative years of his life. Despite the obstacles of his early life, he has achieved enviable personal accomplishments.

---

[24] At the outbreak of WWII, permanent resident aliens of axis countries who were resident in the United States, were classified as "enemy aliens" and/or "alien enemies."

In 1960, after nine years and numerous duty stations in the U.S. Air Force, Staff Sergeant Jacobs was selected for the Airman Education and Commissioning Program at Arizona State University from which he received a BS degree in 1962. That same year he was commissioned as a Second Lieutenant. He served another eleven years in various commissioned assignments, retiring in 1973 as a Major, USAF. During this period he earned an MBA from Arizona State University.

Following his military service, Arthur went on to work as an Industrial Engineer for the Motorola Corporation. He also owned and operated his own management consulting business. In 1977, he joined the faculty of the College of Business, Arizona State University at Tempe, where he taught for twenty years until his retirement in 1997. During the course of his teaching career, Arthur received numerous academic awards and is listed in several of <u>Marquis Who's Who</u> publications.

One action stands out above all others and established a place in history for Arthur D. Jacobs. In 1988, the Civil Liberties Act of 1988 was passed. This Act compensated and apologized to World War II Japanese resident aliens and Japanese Americans who had been evacuated, relocated, or interned during the war. The Act ignored German resident aliens and German-Americans who had been identically treated like Arthur D. Jacobs was at the Crystal City, Texas, internment camp. Arthur filed a constitutional challenge to this Act. His claim was discrimination against himself and others similarly situated solely on the basis of their race and national origin.

The U.S. COURT of Appeals D.C. Circuit, turned down the Jacobs class action lawsuit, on technical grounds. Arthur appealed to the Supreme Court on a *Writ of Certiorari*, but was refused a review by the High Court without comment in

1992. The refusal to review was an unfortunate travesty of justice among many others for, despite the slogan "Equal Justice Under Law" carved in stone over the Supreme Court entrance, less than five percent of *Certiorari* cases appealed to that body are ever heard.

The Jacobs story of the World War II internment of resident German aliens and their American-born families has long been ignored. Similar stories of those interned who were of Japanese descent has attracted widespread publicity, sympathy, financial reparations, and an apology from the U.S. Government. Such preferential treatment on the sole basis of race amounts to no less than blatant discrimination against Arthur D. Jacobs and those similarly situated with him, and is a national disgrace.

Hopefully, history will overcome our nation's current obsession with the alleged victimization of racial minorities to the extent that the wartime suffering of non-minority citizens such as Arthur D. Jacobs and the thousands of others like him will finally be recognized. Fairness and common decency call for it and our nation owes them no less.

William J. Hopwood
Commander, USNR (Ret.)
Miami, Florida
March 5, 1999

The Chronology[25]

Principal Events Relating to This Book

Monday, October 1, 1928

My father, Lambert Dietrich Jacobs, age 20, arrives in New York from Bremen, Germany

Monday, May 6, 1929

My mother, Paulina Sophie Knissel, age 22, arrives in New York from Kaiserslautern, Germany

Thursday, October 1, 1931

My brother, Lambert Walter Jacobs, is born in Brooklyn, New York

---

[25] The author has researched this matter for almost ten years. During this period he has collected more than 10,000 pages of official documents from the FBI, the Immigration and Naturalization Service, the U.S. State Department, the National Archives and Records Administration, and the Staatsarchiv, Ludwigsburg, Germany. These U.S. documents were obtained under the Freedom of Information and Privacy Act. Included in these documents are the FBI files of Lambert D. Jacobs, the father of the author; the author's personal letters written to the Department of Justice in 1944 and 1945; as well as the record of the author's internment in Crystal City and Ellis Island.

Saturday, February 4, 1933

The author, Arthur D. Jacobs, is born in Brooklyn, New York

Friday, September 1, 1939

Germany invades Poland - the Blitzkrieg

Sunday, September 3, 1939

Soviet forces surge into Poland's eastern regions

Saturday, September 9, 1939

My father had read a notice in a newspaper that directed that all male citizens of Germany should appear at the German Consulate for registration. My father appeared at the German Consulate at 17 Battery Place, New York, N.Y. and received a "Gemeldet" stamp in his passport showing that he duly registered. The rationale given by my father for this action is that he was a German citizen and he believed he should comply with the laws.

No doubt, this is the single action, taken by my father, which was the root cause of his ensuing problems.

Sunday, December 7, 1941

The Japanese Empire conducts a sneak attack on Pearl Harbor.

Monday, December 8, 1941

President Franklin Delano Roosevelt declares that a state of war exists between the United States and Japan.

Americans and aliens of German descent are arrested by the FBI and interned by the Immigration and Naturalization Service three days before the United States is at war with Germany.

Thursday, December 11, 1941

Germany and Italy declare war on the United States, and in turn the 77th Congress [of the United States] declares war on the Government of Germany and Italy.

Tuesday, June 15, 1943

An FBI agent accompanied by a detective of the New York Police Department search and ransack our home at 411 Himrod Street, Brooklyn, New York. According to the FBI report of this search, **"No contraband was located as result of the search."**

Thursday, June 17, 1943

The findings of the FBI are discussed with Assistant U.S. Attorney, Matthew T. Fagan. Fagan reserves opinion until a report is submitted.

Tuesday, August 31, 1943

The first known FBI report is issued in the case of my father. This report covers the FBI investigation that began on Saturday, June 12, and continued through Thursday, June 24, 1943. The report notes that on June 15, 1943 the premises of 411 Himrod Street, Brooklyn, New York, were searched and **"No contraband was located as result of the search."**

In addition, the details of this report note that my father, Lambert D. Jacobs, stated that **"he would fight Italy and Japan** [emphasis added]."

Tuesday, September 28, 1943

The FBI receives a letter from U.S. Attorney Matthew T. Fagan, Eastern District of New York. This letter advises the FBI that he, Fagan, had interviewed my father and that my father had advised him that my mother was a patient in the Wyckoff Heights Hospital of Brooklyn, where she had undergone a serious operation. Fagan stated that he examined Jacobs in detail, and that it is his opinion that he is not so dangerous, that this matter can't wait until Mrs. Jacobs is recovered. Fagan deferred the matter.

Monday, November 8, 1943

The FBI discovers that my father's name appeared as No. 885 on the list of applicants for membership in the N.S.D.A.P. [Nazi Party].

Even until this day neither the FBI nor any other government agency has provided evidence that my father was an applicant for membership in the Nazi Party. I have come to the conclusion that my father's name appeared on this list

134

just as my name and the names of millions of others appear on hundreds of junk mailing and organizational lists.

Tuesday, November 9, 1943

Two Special Agents of the FBI search and ransack our home for the second time. Again, the report of findings reads "**No contraband or propaganda material was located as a result of the search conducted, and thereafter the subject executed a statement to the effect that $2.81 was found on the premises during the search.**"

My father voluntarily accompanied the Agents to the office of the FBI's New York Field Division, where he was interrogated and questioned over and over again about his affiliation with the Nazi Party. The FBI report reads that my father "**continuously denied membership in the N.S.D.A.P. [Nazi Party] at any time or any place.**"

Saturday, November 13, 1943

Once again an FBI agent presents my father's case to U.S. Attorney, Matthew T. Fagan. Fagan exams and defers the case until he had a chance to interview my father.

Tuesday, February 15, 1944

The Swedish ship M.S. Gripsholm sets sail for Germany. Aboard are at least 634 German American internees who had been interned at Crystal City Internment Camp, Crystal City, Texas. These internees were to be exchanged for persons of the Americas who were being held in internment by Hitler's Third Reich.   The planning of this exchange voyage had taken place several months before.   Of those being exchanged, 22 percent were males under the age of sixteen, and 19 percent were females also under the age of sixteen. In other words more than 40 percent of those to be exchanged were minors; another 30 percent were adult females; and just over 28 percent were adult males; of those nine were 17 to 20 year olds. Many, if not most of the minor children were American-born.

Replacements for those repatriated on this voyage of the Gripsholm would have to be made available for future exchange voyages the government was planning. Plans for the next exchange voyage got underway as early as **March 1944,** and on **Sunday, January 7, 1945**, the vessel M.S. Gripsholm sailed from Jersey City with 1,043 German repatriates for exchange for persons of the Americas held by the government of the Third Reich.

Friday, February 18, 1944

Government officials question my father almost the entire day. First, he was grilled by an agent of the FBI, then by Matthew T. Fagan, United States Attorney for the Eastern District of New York, in the Federal Building, Brooklyn, New York. The results of these interrogations are reported to the Attorney General ATTN: Honorable Edward J. Ennis, Director Alien Enemy Control Unit as follows:

"Sir:

I examined the above-named subject [LAMBERT DIETRICH JACOBS] at my office today.

He stated that he was born in Germany in 1908; that he came to the United States in 1928; that he made no return trips; that he married in this country in 1930; that there are two children of this marriage, eleven and twelve years of age; that he objects to fighting in the United States Army against either Japan or Germany; that he would not fight against Japan[26] because she is an ally of Germany; that he wants Germany to defeat England because England is a trouble-maker; that he wants Germany to defeat Russia because he does not like Communists; that he understands the defeat of Russia and England by Germany would be against the best interests of the United States but that makes no difference to him; that if in Germany he would fight against the United States because he would have no choice in the matter; that he is **not a member of the Nazi Party** or any other German organization; that he has one war bond in the amount of $25.00 which he purchased through payroll deduction plan at $1.00 per week; **that he wants the United States to win this war; that he does not plan to return to Germany; that his wife does not plan to return to Germany; that the children consider themselves American and have no desire to live in Germany;** that if he were a citizen, he would fight for the United States, but he does not intend to become a citizen until after the war; that his mother and father are presently in Germany; that his married sister resides in Germany and her husband is in the German Army; **that he likes the government of the United States; that he does not care for the present regime in Germany; that he would not care to work in a defense plant [because if there was any sabotage in the defense plant he would be the first to be accused]...that he does not care what happens to Japan.**

---

[26] This statement is in direct contradiction to an August 31, 1943, FBI detailed report which states: "He [Lambert D. Jacobs] stated however, he would fight against Japan and Italy [underline added]."

I am enclosing herewith FBI reports No. 100-49530, dated August 13, 1943, and November 17, 1943.

On the basis of the foregoing, I respectfully request a Presidential Warrant, with interim parole pending hearing before the Board."

Author's notes:

I have compared the foregoing Fagan memorandum to Ennis, with two related FBI documents, (1) a synopsis of an FBI detail report; and (2) the three pages of details of the FBI agent's interrogation of my father. One of the pages is almost completely excised. The excised paragraphs, three of them, contain information provided by a FBI informant. Below these paragraphs is this statement: **"Inquiry at the subject's residence at 411 Himrod Street, Brooklyn, New York, was <u>negative</u> as to information concerning the subject and his wife."** Even though the leads provided by an informant to the FBI proved to be false, the synopsis report, i.e., the report read by decision makers, **did not report that the FBI had been misled by the informant.**

.

Wednesday, February 23, 1944

According to an Edward J. Ennis memorandum, the Presidential Warrant with interim parole was issued to the Federal Bureau of Investigation (FBI).

Wednesday, March 8, 1944

My father is apprehended by the FBI and granted interim parole, pending a hearing before the Alien Enemy Hearing Board.

Friday, March 17, 1944

On this St. Patrick's Day of 1944 the Alien Enemy Hearing Board summons my father for a hearing. I remember my father saying that after this meeting this whole thing with the FBI would be put to rest. Up to a point my father's thinking was correct. My father believed in the American system of justice. My father was confident that once the evidence was heard, that he would be cleared. My mother, my American-born aunt by marriage, and my father's best friend, Dan Lipensky, an American Jew of Russian heritage, are my father's character witnesses at the meeting of the Alien Enemy Hearing Board. After the members of the Hearing Board and U.S. Attorney hear the testimony of my father and his witnesses, the board unanimously agrees that my father should not be interned, but paroled.

Life went on for us after this ordeal. But it was not the same. Each time that there was a knock on our door, my mother would become frightened. Mom expected the FBI agents to be at the door. She had a premonition that the FBI would come and arrest her husband and/or ransack her home again.

The FBI had turned my mother into a nervous wreck. She was never the same after the second FBI ordeal.

Tuesday, October 3, 1944

An agent of the FBI reports that Special Assistant to the Attorney General Robert Hitchcock of the Eastern District of New York declined to prosecute my father. The details of the report read as follows:

> "DETAILS: The facts of this case were presented to Special Assistant to the Attorney General Robert Hitchcock in the Eastern District of New York, who advised that evidence concerning the subject's participation in a conspiracy to violate Section 80, Title 18, United States Code, was insufficient to warrant prosecution and the evidence likewise insufficient to prosecute the subject for violation of Section 80, Title 18 United States Code, in failing to set forth affiliation with the NSDAP [Nazi Party] in his 1942 application for a Certificate of Identification as an Alien Enemy.
>
> Mr. Hitchcock further advised that the Statute of Limitations had run [out] as to any similar violation in connection with his 1940 Alien Registration."

Monday, October 30, 1944

Unbeknownst to either my mother or father on this day, the Attorney General of the United States, Francis Biddle orders my father to be interned. General Biddle issues this order even though my father's Hearing Board recommended that he not be interned. All of us had put this last FBI visit and

Pop's hearing behind us. We thought my father's ordeal was over. Little did we know that the situation would worsen.

Friday, November 3, 1944

This is the day that armed FBI agents raided my father's workplace, handcuffed him and drug him out of the factory. My father later told me he was made to look as if he were a criminal. He was working for the General Diaper Service Division of General Institute of Child Hygiene, at Elmhurst, Long Island, N.Y., a factory I visited several times. Here my father worked as the maintenance engineer for power plant operations and general maintenance—he was a maintenance mechanic. This same day the FBI into the custody of the Immigration and Naturalization Service at Ellis Island, New York Island Harbor, NY, delivered him. At Ellis Island my father immediately advises the officials that at his home there is an emergent condition, namely that his wife was in poor health, and that his two sons were of the age that require the care and protection of their father. My father knew that my mother would be stressed. He knew Mom would be frantic—his thinking was correct.

Then my father proceeded to request that he be interned at the Crystal City Texas Family Internment Camp because (1) he wanted his family with him; (2) of his wife's poor health; and (3) his sons were of the age that required his care and protection.

Saturday, November 4, 1944

The Ellis Island officials (Immigration and Naturalization Service INS officers) notify the Bureau of Public Assistance by telephone of the emergent condition at our home, noted previously, and that my mother only had $2.00. The public

141

assistance office advised the INS official that someone would be sent to our home on Monday, November 6, 1944.

On this same day T. Vincent Quinn, the United States Attorney for the Eastern District of New York writes a letter to the Attorney General of the United States. In this letter Quinn advises the Attorney General that my father, Lambert Dietrich Jacobs had been interned as directed, and then Quinn quoted from the recommendations of the board:

> "His wife [Paula Jacobs] also appeared as witness for him [Lambert Jacobs] and it was brought out that she has been very ill and unable to support her sons. Accordingly, if internment is directed, it would seem appropriate to be necessary that his wife and two children accompany him"

Quinn goes on to say that he, Mr. Quinn, agreed with the Hearing Board's unanimous decision not to intern Lambert Dietrich Jacobs. In other words, Quinn stresses that the Board's decision was unanimous, and that he was in full agreement with the Board's recommendation. Despite being provided with this information, Edward J. Ennis, the director of the Alien Enemy Control Unit, **the judge, jury, and** *executioner,* made the decision to intern my father.

Author's note: I have come to learn that Dan Priest, the Chairman of my father's Alien Enemy Hearing Board was outraged at the decision by the Department of Justice, to intern my father despite the Board's unanimous recommendation that he not be interned. See The Chronology entry date of November 10, 1944.

Monday, November 6, 1944

Finally my mother got word that my father was interned at Ellis Island, New York Harbor, N.Y., and that visitation was permissible on Sundays. My mother was glad to learn that he was okay and so was I.

Wednesday, November 8, 1944

Edward J. Ennis [Director of the Alien Enemy Control Unit, Department of Justice] through C.E. Rhetts an Acting Assistant Attorney General, responds to U.S. Attorney Quinn's letter. In this memorandum Rhetts states, "In reaching the decision that internment was required in this case, stress was placed on the evidence of the subject's [alleged] pro-German sympathies and his [alleged] concealment of his connection with the Nazi Party." I have added the term "alleged" because as the reader will find neither of these statements has been proven.

Friday, November 10, 1944

Daniel Priest, of Milbank, Tweed & Hope, 15 Broad Street, New York 3, NY, the chairman of my father's hearing board learns that the Alien Enemy Control Unit had ignored the Board's recommendation that my father be paroled, and not interned.

Monday, November 13, 1944

In a letter to the Honorable C.E. Rhetts, Acting Assistant Attorney General, Daniel Priest, the chairman of my father's hearing board, writes:

"Upon attending a scheduled meeting of our Hearing Board in Brooklyn on Friday...I was disturbed to learn that our **unanimous** recommendation for parole in the above case [Alien Enemy, Lambert Dietrich Jacobs] had not been followed by your office, but that instead the alien's internment had been ordered.

I suppose it is impossible for you to consult with the Hearing Boards whenever their recommendations are disregarded, but I cannot help thinking that such course should be followed in cases such as this **where so drastic a change has been made in the disposition recommended by a unanimous Board**.

I trust it is not too late to reconsider the internment order and request that the file be re-examined with a view to reinstating our recommendation for parole.

In reaching its conclusion that internment was not required but that parole would sufficiently protect our country's interests, our Board relied very heavily upon impressions received from the extended oral examination of the alien himself and his witnesses. ...if you would talk with this alien, you would agree with us that internment is not the proper disposition of the case.

It is true that the record contains some conflicting statements, particularly as to the extent to which he has foresworn his allegiance to Germany. This discrepancy was given careful consideration by our Board and we felt that the real explanation of his attitude is that he has a certain amount of Teutonic stubbornness and sentimental regard for his Fatherland. He has not been very successful and also has been under the handicap of supporting his invalid wife and two minor sons, both of whom were born in this country....

...One of his other witnesses was Daniel Lipensky, a Russian Jew, who **recommended him without reservation.** Our Board felt that Lipensky, because of his obvious racial prejudice against the Nazis, would have been the first to notice any pro-Hitler sympathy on the part of the subject.

Over and above the apparent injustice to the subject if internment is ordered, the Board believed **that** internment would be a mistake in that it would be necessary in all fairness to intern his semi-invalid wife and two half-grown boys. This...**might also have a bad effect on the future life and attitude of the boys, both of whom are American citizens.**

Another reason for my being disturbed at your decision is that our Board and the other Boards in Brooklyn, as I am informed, having regularly been paroling or releasing aliens of Jacobs' type. Accordingly his internment will be inconsistent with positions heretofore taken and approved by your office...[emphasis added]"

U.S. Attorney Quinn's letter and the cited Priest letter prompted the government action of November 20.

Monday, November 20, 1944

At 9:35 this morning the Alien Enemy Control Unit telephoned EJM[27] of the Immigration and Naturalization office at Ellis Island. EJM then prepared a written memorandum directed to the District Director of the Immigration and Naturalization Service in New York. In this memorandum EJM states that:

> "The Alien Enemy Control Unit advises that the name of the above alien [Lambert D. Jacobs] appears on a list of persons who [allegedly] made application for membership in the Nazi Party subsequent to the year 1939, he being number 885 on the approved list, but the alien denies this.
>
> However, that Unit requests that a statement be taken from Mr. Jacobs in this regard, your office to advise him that his name is on the Nazi Party list, and question him as to why he joined, when he joined, and what he did in it. **In the event the alien is not inclined to discuss the matter, the Alien Enemy Control Unit suggests that he be advised that his continued silence about the matter will only result in the continuation of his internment [emphasis added].**
>
> The Unit requests that your expeditious attention be given to this matter."

---

[27] EJM is not identified in the memorandum, the initials given are the sole identification.

Tuesday, November 21, 1944

Edward J. Ennis, the Director of the Alien Enemy Control Unit, responds to the Priest letter of November 13. Ennis' response required one and one half single spaced pages and in it Ennis attempts to justify the position taken by the Alien Enemy Control Unit. His response to Mr. Priest follows:

"I have your letter of November 13 to Mr. Rhetts requesting that the decision of internment in this case [Lambert Dietrich Jacobs] be reconsidered in the light of the Board's recommendation of parole. **I shall be glad to have the case reviewed completely.** I think that you will be interested in the considerations of which we applied to the case upon the original decision of internment.

It was noted that the Board stated that a year ago its recommendation would be internment in the case but they considered the case from all angles at the present time and because of the comparatively recent changes in the general situation, parole was recommended. It appeared, therefore, to us that the case was one of some doubt in the minds of the members of the Board and that if the subject had revealed his [alleged] connection with the Nazi Party in his registration [alien enemy registration] and then had been apprehended at the beginning of the war, the Board would certainly have recommended his internment. **Of course, we are not interning all members or all applicants for membership in the Nazi Party...**

In very many cases repeated denials of membership have been finally followed by admissions and we have accepted the admission as some indication of a willingness to depart from a strict adherence to domination by the German government so that parole

147

is warranted. In cases where individuals have persisted in denying any connection with the Party, however, as in this case, it has been the practice to order internment unless there is no other adverse evidence at all and there are present strong mitigating circumstances..."

Author's note: Mr. Ennis makes a compelling statement to Priest, but **Ennis did not tell Priest the "rest of the story"** and/or **what he, Ennis, did/does behind closed doors.**

The following is a synopsis as to what neither the FBI reports nor Mr. Ennis told Priest: (1) The case against my father is weak; (2) my father duly registered as an alien both in 1940 and 1942; and (3) most significant on October 16, 1940 my father registered under the Selective Training and Service Act of 1940 with his local Draft Board #221 in Brooklyn, New York; (4) as of April 22, 1941 my father's Draft Board classified him as "3" for the draft; (5) my father did not claim any exemptions with his Draft Board; and (6) on April 20, 1938 my father filed a "Declaration of Intention" to become a citizen of the United States, and is so recorded in Vol. 413438, Certificate #2-82711.

Furthermore, it is important for the reader to understand some of the practices of Ennis while in the Department of Justice. At 4:25 P.M. on **Friday, May 21, 1943,** a conversation between a Captain Hall (a member of the Staff Judge Advocate's office of the U.S. Army), and Mr. Edward J. Ennis regarding the disposition of the case of Olga Schueller, age 53. Mrs. Schueller a German-born American citizen, naturalized in 1920, defied an order of the United States Army that directed her to leave the Eastern Defense Area. Mrs. Schueller had two sons, one in the United States Navy and the other worked in an important defense plant. In addition the conversation also involved the so-called Ebel case. Both cases concern the exclusion of citizens from certain defense areas.

Mr. Ennis and Captain Hall during this conversation were scheming to "trick" the court in both the Schueller and Ebel cases. The discussion is about tricking the court. Ennis and Hall want to get a three-judge court "stacked" in their favor. The following statement summarizes Ennis' thoughts (on page 6 of the transcript): "**Oh sure. All three district judges, John [Captain Hall], are just dying to do their patriotic duty for the country. They just fall right into your lap. It's disgusting** [underscore added]."

Thursday, November 23, 1944 *Thanksgiving Day*

Armand J. Salturelli, a District Parole Officer of the New York Immigration and Naturalization Office interrogates my father. In his report of November 28, 1944, Salturelli notes:

> "He was questioned extensively concerning his [membership in the Nazi Party] but repeatedly denied that he was ever an applicant or a member of this party.
>
> During the course of the interview he was advised that the records of the Department of Justice had indicated that his name appeared as #885 on the approved list of Nazi Party applicants or members. However, his only answer to this was that he was at a loss to understand how his name ever appeared on such a list. He was also advised that his continued silence concerning his association with the Nazi Party would in all probability result in the continuation of his internment and to this he only reiterated that he was telling the truth and that at no time did he ever

make application or was he ever a member of the Nazi Party."

Thursday, November 30, 1944

Daniel Lipensky, a American Jew of Russian heritage, my father's best friend writes a letter to Evelyn M. Hersey, Assistant to the Commissioner of the Immigration and Naturalization Service.

In this letter Lipensky states:

> *"I am writing this letter with the hope that it will help in the reconsideration and I hope his [Lambert Jacobs] release. I am writing about Lambert Jacobs who is being held at Ellis Island as a dangerous alien I presume, but it's wrong.*
>
> *I am an American Jew and I certainly have no use for the Nazis. I feel that there must be some mistake for his being held. I have known Mr. Jacobs and his family about 10 years, I have never known him to do or say anything wrong, on the contrary, he would often go out of his way to help a fellow. I know that his children were and are being brought up as real Americans.*
>
> *I know that Mr. Jacobs was never in favor of the present government in Germany. I have known him long before the war. I have found him to be a man of fine character.*
>
> *I know that he appreciates and loves the U.S.A. for the opportunities and freedom that America affords.*

I know that his wife is not well and not able to support herself and her children from what they receive from the welfare department, they need him home badly for morale and as a breadwinner.

Never being separated from one another I think it is a hard blow. I hate to think of them separated for Christmas; the children always looked forward to that holiday.

Somehow I feel an injustice is being done. I know that when you reconsider this case you will find that Lambert Jacobs is not a dangerous alien."

Monday, December 11, 1944

Mrs. Violet Knissel, a witness before my father's Hearing Board writes Ennis:

"I am writing in regards to Mr. Lambert Jacobs who is interned at Ellis Island.

I am an American Born Citizen and cannot see why Mr. Jacobs has been taken away from his family. As he is in every way just as good an American as many a born one.

I have known him for a good many years and in all that time he always lived the American way and brought his two boys up - as all American boys.

His family needs him very badly at home as the mother is sick and cannot do anything to help support them. The children are fast growing boys and their

151

mother needs plenty of money to clothe and feed them properly.

I do wish you would reconsider his case and let a man who has done no wrong to return to his family."

Tuesday, December 12, 1944

My brother and I write a letter to Edward J. Ennis, Director of the Alien Enemy Control Unit of the Department of Justice. We write:

"We cannot do without our father, Lambert D. Jacobs. Our father never refused to let us buy War Bonds and Savings Stamps or to collect paper. We collected 3 tons of paper during our school hours. We cannot manage without our father. My mother cannot do heavy work. Since she had her three operations in one.

We would like to have our father home with us or we be with him in a family camp. We should think that we are Boy Scouts of America and we are American Citizens and we have to do with a certain amount of money. We do not think that it is right to do this to American Citizens.

Arthur D. Jacobs - Age 11
Lambert W. Jacobs - Age 13"

Friday, December 15, 1944

Fred Pardy our landlord at 411 Himrod Street in Brooklyn wrote the following to Edward J. Ennis the Director of the Alien Enemy Control Unit of the Department Justice.

"I am an American born citizen writing to you in reference of Mr. Lambert Jacobs who is interned at Ellis Island. I do not know why you took this man away from his family. We are neighbors and lived in the same house for five years.

I never heard Mr. Jacobs discuss Europe affairs or American politics. He raised his family the American way. The boys are very active toward helping the United States win this war. The boys run around the neighborhood collecting newspaper and they also are boy scouts.

Mrs. Jacobs had an operation about a year ago and it left her in a weakened condition. I am sure if she were able to work she would support the children and also help the war effort. I think that Mr. Jacobs should be home with his family because he is a hard working man and will work at anything.

I do hope that you reconsider Mr. Jacobs' case. I want to thank you."

Wednesday, January 10, 1945

My father writes his former boss, Mr. Holly, Chief Engineer of the General Institute of Child Hygiene at Elmhurst, Long Island, N.Y. In this letter my father writes:

"Just a few words to let you know that I am still detained here at Ellis Island. Although I tried to get back to work for you, my efforts so far have been unsuccessful. Perhaps you could address:

> *Mr. Edward J. Ennis, Director*
> *Alien Control Unit, F.B.I.*
> *Washington, D.C.*

on my behalf, since I am anxious to get back to the job and to my family.

Hoping that you had a cheerful Christmas and with belated wishes for a "Happy New Year"

P.S. Please give my regards to all the boys."

Monday, January 15, 1945

Mr. Adelbert Holly, Chief Engineer of the General Institute of Child Hygiene, writes a letter to Edward J. Ennis, Director of the Alien Enemy Control Unit, Department of Justice. Holly writes:

> *"Enclosed please find a letter I received from Lambert Jacobs.*
>
> *I do not know anything about Mr. Jacobs' private life or your case with him.*
>
> *The year and half that he worked under my supervision is all I know of him.*
>
> *He was satisfactory in all respects, a hard, willing worker and got along well with the other workers.*

On account of labor shortages he would work as many hours as he wished and did work about [illegible] hours for 7 days weekly.

He learned power plant work and general maintenance readily and was very useful to us.

If he was available I would be glad to have him back in our plant.

Hoping this may be of some help in judging his case."

Thursday, January 25, 1945

Ennis replied to all of the letters he received on behalf and in support of my father's release from internment. An example of Ennis' typical response follows:

> "While it is not contemplated that any change will be made at this time in Mr. Jacobs' internment status, your letter will be made part of the file for consideration in the event that his case is re-examined at a later date."

Saturday, January 27, 1945

I write a second letter to Mr. Ennis:

> *"The reason I am writing this letter to you is because I did not hear anything new on my father's case.*
>
> *My mother was sick in bed last week and it is hard for my brother and me without our father.*

I am sending you two Commendation cards I received from the Principal of the School. Last week I brought a radio to school for the War Veterans to learn to be a Radio Technician.

I think it is a shame to do a thing like this to a father of two American boys who has always let us help the War Effort.

P.S. Please send the commendation cards back. Thank you!"

Tuesday, February 27, 1945

Philip Forman, Chief, Detention and Deportation Section, Ellis Island, 4, New York Harbor, writes in a memorandum to the Assistant Commissioner for Alien Control, Central Office:

> SOPHIE PAULA JACOBS [my mother], wife of the above named [Lambert Jacobs], appeared at this station and stated that she had disposed of all her home furnishings and had nowhere to reside with her two children. Pursuant to the telephonic authority received from Mr. Collaer they were permitted to remain at this station..."

Thursday, April 26, 1945

Under escort of an Immigration and Naturalization Service "guard and matron" the Jacobs family departs Ellis Island for the Crystal City Family Internment Camp, Crystal City, Texas. Rail transportation is the mode of transport used.

Sunday, April 29, 1945

The Jacobs family arrives and is detained in the Crystal City Internment Camp, Crystal City, Texas.

Monday, May 7, 1945

Germany is defeated and surrenders unconditionally to the United States and its allies.

Saturday, July 14, 1945

The President of the United States, Harry S. Truman, proclaims that:

> "All alien enemies now or hereinafter interned within the continental limits of the United States...shall be deemed by the Attorney General to be dangerous to the public peace and safety of the United States...shall be subject upon the order of the Attorney General to removal from the United States and may be required to depart therefrom in accordance with such regulations as he may prescribe."

Tuesday, August 7, 1945

According to the aforementioned proclamation the Honorable Herbert Wechsler, Assistant Attorney General, notifies my father that it has been determined that he will be removed from the United States and repatriated to the country of his nationality.

Sunday, September 2, 1945

Japan defeated.

Monday, October 1, 1945

The fourteenth birthday of the author's brother Lambert W. Jacobs.

Monday, October 8, 1945

Because of the threat of deportation my father volunteers to be repatriated to Germany; my mother agrees to be repatriated with my father. In addition my parents note that they wanted my brother and me to be repatriated [expatriated] with them.

Friday, November 9, 1945

The Honorable Tom C. Clark, Attorney General of the United States, orders that my father depart the United States within thirty days of this notice.

Saturday, December 1, 1945

Along with ninety-seven other internees, the Jacobs family leaves the Crystal City Family Internment Camp, Crystal Texas. This group of 101 repatriates is transported under armed guard via rail to Ellis Island, New York Harbor, N.Y.

Tuesday, December 4, 1945

The Jacobs family is received and interned at Ellis Island, New York Harbor, N.Y.

Thursday, January 17, 1946

The Jacobs family departs Ellis Island and boards the S.S. Aiken Victory, destination Bremerhaven, Germany—to a war-torn and starving land. The Immigration and Naturalization Service notifies the FBI and other interested departments that the Jacobs left the United States.

Sunday, January 27, 1946

The S.S. Aiken Victory docks in Bremerhaven Germany. The Jacobs family and the other internees are greeted by a band of armed soldiers of the United States Army.

This same day this group of internees is transported under armed guards in U.S. Army trucks to Bremen, Germany.

Monday, January 28, 1946

At Bremen, Germany the group is loaded into boxcars [cattle cars or viehwagen as they are called in German] and transported also under armed guards to Ludwigsburg, Germany. **Our diet for the next ninety-two hours would be <u>bread and water</u>. Our toilet facility inside the boxcar, during this same period, was an open stinking bucket.**

Thursday, January 31, 1946

My father, brother and I were taken to Hohenasperg in the vicinity of Ludwigsburg, Germany. The official U.S. Army title for this camp is Camp 76, Seventh Army Internment Camp. It was a 15th Century citadel. In essence this was a prison, operated by the U.S. Seventh Army, for high-ranking German officers suspected of war crimes. This facility was heavily armed and we were closely guarded and placed into separate cells.

My mother was taken to another camp, Camp 77 also a Seventh Army internment camp, but this camp was for females and their young children. **My brother and I were not considered young children.**

Monday, February 4, 1946

This is thirteenth birthday of the author, Arthur D. Jacobs.

Thursday, February 7, 1946

It is presumed that an official learns that my brother and I were American citizens and that we should not be imprisoned at this god-forsaken place. We were transferred to another camp somewhere in Ludwigsburg, Germany.

Friday, March 15, 1946

My father is released from Camp 76 [Hohenasperg, Germany]. My mother is released from Camp 77 [Ludwigsburg, Germany] **"Free" at last**.

160

Saturday, December 28, 1946

Some time before this date my brother and I reported to the American Consulate to advise the consulate that we are American citizens and are in need of a passport to identify ourselves, and that we may use it to return home to the United States of America.

On this day the official records of the United States Department of State reflects that my brother and I were issued a passport. However, we did not receive this passport. Thus, we still had no proof that we were, in fact, American citizens.

Friday, October 17, 1947

The American Consulate at Bremen, Germany issues Passport No. 928, FS 180733, Service No. 6169 to my brother, Lambert Walter Jacobs and to myself, Arthur Dietrich Jacobs.

Wednesday, October 29, 1947

My brother and I set sail from Bremen, Germany aboard the Marine Flasher—destination the United States of America. Our parents remain in Germany.

Sunday, November 10, 1947

The Immigration and Naturalization Service admit my brother and me back into our country, the United States of America, at the Port of New York.

June 1958

I see my parents for the first time since I left them in November 1947.